MARY
HANDMAID OF THE LORD

MARY
HANDMAID OF THE LORD

Geoff Henstock

THE CHRISTADELPHIAN
404 Shaftmoor Lane
Hall Green
Birmingham B28 8SZ

2010

First published 2010

ISBN 978-0-85189-190-3

Printed and bound in Malta by:
GUTENBERG PRESS LIMITED

CONTENTS

PREFACE

THIS book seeks to direct our minds to an extraordinary sister – Mary: the handmaid of the Lord – in the hope that the reader will come to know Mary better and come to admire her. We shall find inspiring examples of faithfulness in her life; these offer instruction and exhortation for our walk as brothers and sisters of her son.

It is a sad fact that false Christianity has promoted a corrupted picture of Mary. There is a term – Mariolatry – to describe the idolatrous worship of this very special woman. In Roman Catholic churches and homes around the world there are pictures, icons and statues of Mary; she has been elevated to a position of honour that rivals even that of her son, the Lord Jesus Christ.

Such excesses and perversions may have tended to make some Christadelphians recoil from Mary. Within our community we do not often speak about Mary and it is possible that we do not always recognise as we ought her very special position in God's redemptive plan. The divine estimation of this holy woman, however, is that Mary is "highly favoured" and "blessed ... among women!" (Luke 1:28).

This study has drawn upon the thoughts of many speakers and authors. A select bibliography lists some of the sources that were found to be particularly helpful, but there are many other works and individuals that contributed ideas and impressions which have been drawn upon in the preparation of this book.

1

MARY OF NAZARETH

"But when the fulness of the time had come, God sent forth his Son, born of a woman." (Galatians 4:4)

DARKNESS reigned in Israel for more than 400 years, during which time God did not reveal Himself openly to His people. By the time the Herod family came to power many sectors of Jewish society had become corrupt and Greek philosophy and other Gentile influences had tainted the purity of Jewish religion and worship. In spite of this, as in the days of Elijah when there were 7,000 who had not bowed unto Baal, there were many individuals and families who retained a vibrant and pure faith. They yearned for the promised deliverance of the nation, for the fulfilment of the promises to the patriarchs, for the coming of Messiah and for the "restitution of all things", the re-establishment of the kingdom of God on earth. In the days of Herod those waiting for the "consolation of Israel" were about to be rewarded for their faithful endurance. Their waiting was about to end.

A virgin

Human reasoning might expect that divine intervention in the affairs of men should be accompanied by dramatic events and circumstances. Sometimes it is, as in the flood in the days of Noah, but often it is not. The God of earthquake, wind and fire is also the God of the still small voice, and it is in that quiet and unobtrusive form that divine intervention often takes place. Such was the case in Galilee in the days of Herod.

Gabriel was sent to a virgin in Nazareth. Gabriel, whose name means 'man of God', was sent to foreshadow the coming of the one who would be Son of man and Son of God. He was sent to a Galilean virgin; the word 'virgin' (Greek, *parthenos*), means just that – a chaste, unmarried woman. The word suggests nothing about Mary's age. The same word is used of Mary in Matthew 1:23, where the record quotes Isaiah 7:14. In that passage in Isaiah, King Ahaz was given a sign:

> "Therefore the Lord himself will give you a sign: Behold, the virgin shall conceive and bear a son, and shall call his name Immanuel."

A virgin would conceive and bear a son. This would, of course, require a miracle such as that described in Luke 1. The child's name 'Immanuel' is symbolic, meaning 'God with us', hinting at the fact that God was to be the father. The mother was to be a virgin (Hebrew, *alma*) which literally means a woman of marriageable age.

Technically the word *alma* only applies to age rather than morality; unlike the Greek *parthenos* it does not necessarily imply a chaste woman of marriageable age. But everywhere *alma* is used in the Bible it does refer to a virgin of marriageable age[1]. The Septuagint uses the word *parthenos* in this verse and the fact that the prophecy is quoted in Matthew 1, when Mary's betrothed husband Joseph is reassured about the integrity of his wife-to-be, proves that Mary is the fulfilment of this prophecy.

If the Hebrew word *alma* means a woman of marriageable age, what did that mean at that time? Almost certainly it meant she was a teenager, perhaps between fourteen and sixteen, but maybe as young as twelve. It was considered the duty of every Israelite to marry as early in life as possible. Young Jewish men at this time were meant to marry at about sixteen or seventeen, and certainly no later than twenty.[2] The Books of 1 and 2 Kings record several cases of kings of

---

1 – See, for example, Genesis 24:43, Exodus 2:8, Proverbs 30:19.
2 – Alfred Edersheim, *Sketches of Jewish Social Life in the Days of Christ*, page 147.

2

Judah who fathered sons while still in their teens. Ancient Rabbis said that anyone unmarried after his twentieth year was cursed of God. If he refused to marry after that age he could even be forced by a court to be married! Jewish parents were encouraged to give their children in marriage as soon as they reached puberty, and while marriage was not as stringently enforced for girls they were strongly advised to marry to avoid suspicion about their moral integrity[3].

Who was this virgin to whom Gabriel was sent? For reasons explained in the next chapter, it is not possible to be certain about Mary's genealogy. Most of what we know for certain about Mary's background is found in Luke 1. Our first encounter with this woman is in verse 27:

"Now in the sixth month the angel Gabriel was sent by God to a city of Galilee named Nazareth, to a virgin betrothed to a man whose name was Joseph, of the house of David. The virgin's name was Mary."

(Luke 1:26,27)

Mary was betrothed to Joseph. The word "betrothed" is used only three times (once in Matthew 1:18, here, and in Luke 2:5) and always of Mary; it means 'promised in marriage'. Jewish parents often promised their daughters in marriage while still infants, and could do so up to the age of twelve years and a day. They were forbidden to marry their daughter to the man to whom they betrothed her until she reached puberty, which could be as early as twelve. At some stage in her early life, therefore, it would seem that Mary had been promised to Joseph.

To people living in affluent western societies today it is confronting – perhaps even morally repugnant – to think of a girl in her early teens being married and caring for children. We are unwise, however, to judge the actions of parents in another age and society by the mores of modern western society. Marriage at such a

---

3 – *The Jewish Encyclopedia*, Volume VIII, page 347, Article Marriage Laws, Funk & Wagnalls, 1916.

young age seems inappropriate to most people in the western world, but in many other parts of the world different standards apply. In the Middle East to this day, for instance, Bedouin women still marry in their early to mid teens and there are other societies where this remains the norm.

There are others who struggle to believe that Mary was a teenager when Gabriel came to her because of her evident maturity and the advanced spirituality she manifests in the Song of Mary.[4] The question of maturity may be discounted because Mary lived in a society that expected females of that age to be ready for marriage and they were brought up with that expectation. Mary's extraordinary spirituality is somewhat harder to explain. Presumably it reflects at least in part the influence of her parents, but we should also bear in mind that her song was a divinely inspired declaration, which may account in large degree for the remarkable nature of the passage.

An orphan?

The Mary we encounter in Luke 1 then is probably a girl no older than mid teens. It is quite possible that Mary was an orphan, for in Luke 1:56, after an extended stay with her relative Elizabeth, she returned to Nazareth to what the Bible very precisely describes as "her house". Single women did not usually live alone at this time. They lived with their parents or, if older and unmarried, with another male relative. In Bethany, for instance, Mary and her sister Martha lived with their brother Lazarus. Women who lived alone in ancient Israel often were regarded as having dubious morals.

The fact that a teenager, who was betrothed and not yet married, returned to her own house and not that of her parents or her brother suggests that she had been orphaned and was alone in the world. Be that as it may,

4 – Lilian Adams makes this case in *The Testimony*, Volume 10 (1940), pages 95,96,100.

we may be certain that Mary and her betrothed husband were poor. This is clear from Luke 2:22-24, where details are provided of the offering made following the birth of Jesus:

"Now when the days of her purification according to the law of Moses were completed, they brought him to Jerusalem to present him to the Lord (as it is written in the law of the Lord, 'Every male who opens the womb shall be called holy to the Lord'), and to offer a sacrifice according to what is said in the law of the Lord, 'A pair of turtledoves or two young pigeons.'"

A pair of turtledoves, or two young pigeons was the offering of the very poorest people in Israel (Leviticus 12:6-8). Even after having married Joseph, therefore, Mary was still poor.

Miriam

Mary is the Greek form of the Hebrew name Miriam. The meaning of 'Miriam' is unflattering. Strong says it means "rebellious", while Gesenius says it means "their contumacy (i.e., insolence)". Young says it means "fat, thick, strong". Perhaps these meanings, along with the example of Miriam, explain why there was only one woman named Miriam in the Old Testament!

The Greek version of the name, 'Mary', on the other hand, was very common among the Jews in the land at the time of Christ. It was not the sister of Moses that people had in mind, however, when they used this name in the time of Jesus. It is thought that the name was so popular because of the strong affection at that time for a beautiful Hasmonean princess of that name. Up to seven women bore this name in the New Testament.

Regardless of why her parents might have called their daughter Mary, it is likely that a woman as spiritually alert as the mother of Jesus would have contemplated any similarities that might have existed between her and Miriam of the Exodus record. This might be so especially in the weeks and months after

5

she was informed she would bear a child who would be called Jesus – 'Yahweh shall save'. There are several intriguing parallels:

- Miriam was divinely ordained to protect the infant Moses. When Moses was consigned to a basket floating in the reeds beside the Nile it was "his sister" (almost certainly Miriam) who watched over him (Exodus 2:3,4).

- When Pharaoh's daughter found the babe it was "his sister" who intervened to ensure that a faithful Hebrew woman was assigned the task of nurturing Israel's future deliverer (Exodus 2:7,8). It is thought that Miriam was about ten at this time, only a few years younger than Mary was when she gave birth to Jesus. Neither Mary nor Miriam allowed their youth to impede the discharge of their spiritual responsibilities.

- Miriam was a prophetess who spoke of God's triumph over the power of sin (Exodus 15:20,21); sentiments echoed in the Song of Mary.

- Like Mary in relation to Jesus, Miriam initially was supportive of Moses in his work as deliverer of the people (Exodus 15:20), but in later years she struggled to appreciate fully the nature of that work and resisted him. Mary's resistance took the form of seeking to dissuade Jesus from the discharge of his duties, whereas Miriam's resistance was much more serious and took the form of open rebellion against Moses (Numbers 12).

Some of these parallels might not have seemed immediately obvious to Mary as she contemplated her position as the maidservant of the Lord during her pregnancy, but in later years she may have had cause to consider their relevance to her own life. The record in Numbers 12 may have been especially challenging to Mary.

Paul appears to allude to Miriam's challenge to Moses when writing to the Corinthians about the role of sisters in the ecclesia:

"Let your women keep silent in the churches, for
they are not permitted to speak; but they are to be
submissive, as the law also says. And if they want to
learn something, let them ask their own husbands at
home; for it is shameful for women to speak in
church. Or did the word of God originally come from
you? Or was it you only that it reached?"

(1 Corinthians 14:34-36)

It has been suggested[5] that verse 36, designed to
underline the force of the command in verses 34 and 35,
could be an ironic reversal of the question posed by
Miriam when she and Aaron challenged Moses:

"Then Miriam and Aaron spoke against Moses ...
So they said, 'Has the LORD indeed spoken only
through Moses? Has he not spoken through us also?'"

(Numbers 12:1,2)

That Miriam is named first suggests that she took the
lead in challenging Moses. Paul's words in 1
Corinthians 14:37 also appear to echo the language of
God in Numbers 12:6.

1 Corinthians 14:37	Numbers 12:6
"If anyone thinks himself to be a prophet or spiritual, let him acknowledge that the things which I write to you are the commandments of the Lord."	"Then he said, 'Hear now my words: If there is a prophet among you, I, the LORD, make myself known to him in a vision; I speak to him in a dream.'"

Mary would have been conscious of the divine favour
bestowed upon her and perhaps of the fact that in the
Song of Mary she had uttered divinely inspired words,
making her, like Miriam, a prophetess. Such an
experience must have a profound effect upon any man
or woman. In these circumstances it is possible that

5 – In *Christadelphian eJournal of Biblical Interpretation*, Volume
2, No. 2, April 2008, pages 21-23.

Mary might have imagined she had a right to suggest to her son an alternative course of action to that being pursued at the time, in particular one that did not involve so much risk for him and sacrifice for her personally. This may be the sentiment which underlies the incidents in Luke 2:48,49 and Matthew 12:46-50, when Mary is seen to oppose the discharge of the Lord's duty to his Heavenly Father. Paul found it necessary to provide instruction for unruly prophetesses in Corinth; so our Lord was required to rebuke, albeit quite gently, his mother.

Despised Nazareth

Mary lived in Nazareth, a relatively remote town in Galilee. Galilee was a fertile and scenic region, although Nazareth being located in an upland valley was a little less fertile than lower parts of the region. Nazareth is never mentioned by name in the Old Testament[6] and there are no references to the town in the writings of Josephus, a fact which confirms almost certainly that it was an obscure and unimportant village. It was only one day's journey from the Mediterranean coast, Capernaum and Tiberias and three days' journey from Jerusalem, but no main thoroughfare passed directly through the village.

While Josephus is silent about Nazareth, ancient Rabbinical writings make reference to the town as one of the towns where priests lived when not on duty in the Temple in Jerusalem – no doubt regarding it like a country retreat. Perhaps this explains how Mary could have a cousin in the person of Elizabeth who was of the tribe of Levi. Perhaps it also explains how the religious rulers in Jerusalem came to have such intimate knowledge of the allegations of illegitimacy surrounding the birth of Jesus. It is curious to speculate what impression the resident priests may have had on

---

6 – Alfred Edersheim suggests that Nazareth was "probably the ancient Sarid (or En-Sarid), which, in the time of Joshua, marked the northern boundary of Zebulun (Joshua 19:10,11)". *The Life and Times of Jesus The Messiah*, page 71, but the evidence is scant.

the young Jesus. Almost certainly they would have overseen the education of the boys of the town. Through those priests Jesus probably had first-hand experience of the deadening, demoralised spirituality that sapped so much of the religious vigour from Jewish society in his day.

Some commentators have suggested that Nazareth was a place of considerable significance, perhaps having a population in excess of 10,000. They cite the fact that the New Testament always refers to the place as a city (Greek, *polis*, which strictly signifies 'a walled town') rather than a village (Greek, *kome*, signifying 'an unwalled country town') as evidence of its relative importance. Perhaps it would be reasonable to speculate, therefore, that the use by the Gospel writers of the word 'city' is a mark of respect rather than a denominator of size.

That Mary's home town was a place of little or no consequence in Israel may be implied from Nathanael's guileless question: "Can anything good come out of Nazareth?" (John 1:46). The region of Galilee was spurned and despised by the Jewish elite. They had unmitigated contempt for country people in general and in particular for those from Galilee. The fact that Jesus was born in this region was used to disparage his authority later in his ministry, so despised was Galilee. In John 7:52 the chief priests and Pharisees taunted Nicodemus with the words: "Are you also of Galilee? Search and look, for no prophet has arisen out of Galilee". In fact they were not strictly correct in this regard, for the prophet Jonah hailed from Gath Hepher (2 Kings 14:25), a village remarkably close to Nazareth. Their blind prejudice was not troubled by facts, however, and all through his life they tried to denigrate Jesus because of his rustic origins in Nazareth.

When our Lord was crucified the sign above him described him as, "Jesus of Nazareth, the king of the Jews" (John 19:19). The Jewish rulers tried to have the inscription changed to the effect that Jesus only

9

claimed to be king of the Jews: presumably they were more than happy to leave the first part of the message about his Nazarene origin, thinking that it served to undermine his credibility.

It is surely significant that Almighty God chose a poor family living in an obscure and despised place, remote from the centre of national life in Jerusalem, for His Son's upbringing. God knew that an upbringing among simple country folk and in touch with the rhythms of nature was more suitable for Jesus than an upbringing in the sophisticated courts of Jerusalem. His childhood in Nazareth must have equipped Jesus to understand and relate to the challenges of ordinary men and women and the pressures that come with poverty and with being a social outcast. Paul told the Corinthians that "not many mighty, not many noble, are called" (1 Corinthians 1:26); these are the very people to whom our Lord can readily relate, partly because they include the people among whom he grew up and who constituted his immediate earthly family.

There were many poor villages in Israel, but the location of Nazareth was ideal for the nurturing of the Son of God. While relatively secluded it was still close to many sites associated with Israel's history. George Adam Smith draws attention to this:

"The village lies on the most southern of the ranges of Lower Galilee, and on the edge of this just above the Plain of Esdraelon. You cannot see the surrounding country, for Nazareth rests in a basin among hills; but the moment you climb to the edge of this basin, which is everywhere within the limit of the village boys' playground, what a view you have! Esdraelon lies before you, with its twenty battlefields – the scenes of Barak's and of Gideon's victories, the scenes of Saul's and Josiah's defeats, the scenes of the struggles for freedom in the glorious days of the Maccabees. There is Naboth's vineyard and the place of Jehu's revenge upon Jezebel; there Shunem and the house of Elisha; there Carmel and the place of

Elijah's sacrifice. To the east the Valley of Jordan, with the long range of Gilead; to the west the radiance of the Great Sea, with the ships of Tarshish and the promise of the Isles. You see thirty miles in three directions. It is a map of Old Testament history."[7]

Our Lord's deep and close relationship with his heavenly Father was fundamental to his spiritual development. His childhood and youth in such a location, however, must have served to heighten his spiritual awareness. The Old Testament came alive every time he walked to some secluded elevation to commune with his Father in prayer. And he did this daily for nearly thirty years before he left to commence his public ministry. As this was the place where Mary had been brought up we may assume that she too had benefited spiritually from the proximity of so many significant sites.

We can imagine the pressures Mary would have experienced as an unmarried teenage mother-to-be in a small rural village, especially one where legalistic priests may have exercised considerable influence. She would not be the first local girl to find herself in this situation, but she knew that she was completely innocent of any wrong-doing and had good reason to doubt whether Joseph would stand by her as he most surely would have done had he been the father. It is difficult enough in any society for an unmarried teenager expecting a child but the challenge Mary faced was hard, especially if she had no family to plead her case or protect her from lurid insinuations. Fortunately Mary was not left to face that trial alone: the God of Israel, who is guardian of all the fatherless and the widows, would not have ignored the needs of this orphan.

God gave Mary an angelic message of reassurance at the time of her conception, and perhaps further such

7 – George Adam Smith, *The Historical Geography of the Holy Land*, page 282.

angelic reassurance at later stages in her life. Of course the revealed word of God, with which she was very familiar, also would have afforded Mary much comfort during her difficult life.

Many of the Psalms must have resonated strongly with Mary as she faced the pressures that came upon her. Psalm 22, so clearly messianic, would have given Mary insight into some of the trials that were to envelop her son. Even though it is written from the perspective of her son, Mary as an expectant mother may well have drawn strength from the words of verse 10:

"I was cast upon you from birth. From my mother's womb you have been my God."[8]

These words would have reassured her that God would not abandon her during the days of her confinement, days which must have become progressively more difficult and anxious as the day of the Lord's birth drew near. As her pregnancy advanced Mary would become the subject of more whisperings and unjustified allegations. The words of Psalm 31:17-20 may have strengthened her to endure the attacks of the gossips:

"Do not let me be ashamed, O LORD, for I have called upon you; let the wicked be ashamed; let them be silent in the grave. Let the lying lips be put to silence, which speak insolent things proudly and contemptuously against the righteous. Oh, how great is your goodness, which you have laid up for those who fear you, which you have prepared for those who trust in you in the presence of the sons of men! You shall hide them in the secret place of your presence from the plots of man: you shall keep them secretly in a pavilion from the strife of tongues."

Similarly, Psalm 37:5-6 must have reassured her in times of doubt and anxiety:

---

8 – Similar words are used of the Messiah in Isaiah 49:1: "The LORD has called me from the womb; from the womb of my mother he has made mention of my name."

"Commit your way to the LORD, trust also in him, and he shall bring it to pass. He shall bring forth your righteousness as the light, and your justice as the noonday."

For Mary these were more than just solemn words. She experienced the reality of these wonderful promises in her life. Cruel slander and innuendo by those who had reason thirty years later to try to discredit Jesus would continue to be promulgated all her life, but those closest to her came to realise the truth about her situation. In those initial weeks following her encounter with Gabriel, God provided a secret "pavilion from the strife of tongues" through the haven and valuable support Mary found in the home of her kinswoman Elizabeth. And through His providence God had already provided a husband with a character to meet the challenges they would share as husband and wife as guardians of the Son of God.

2

GENEALOGY OF MARY AND OF JESUS

"... endless genealogies, which cause disputes ..."

TWO separate genealogical records of the Lord Jesus Christ are given: in Matthew 1 and Luke 3. The genealogy of the Lord Jesus Christ may provide interesting detail about Mary's background if we could be certain which of these applies to Mary.

It is commonly said that the genealogy in Matthew is the genealogy of Joseph while the Luke record is that of Mary. That is the view of John Thomas,[9] Robert Roberts,[10] and of James Carter,[11] and it might be so. The tradition that the Luke genealogy is that of Mary dates only from the fifteenth century. Another much older tradition, which dates from the third century, holds that both the Matthew and Luke genealogies are those of Joseph.[12] This view is regarded by Alfred Edersheim as "the more likely".[13]

Frank Jannaway[14] curiously reverses John Thomas' and Robert Roberts' approach and suggests that the Matthew record is the genealogy of Mary while the Luke record is that of Joseph. That view is shared by

9 – John Thomas, *Herald of the Future Age*, Volume 3, page 34 (January 1847).

10 – Robert Roberts, *Nazareth Revisited*, pages 44,45.

11 – James Carter, *The Testimony*, Volume 41 (1971), pages 277,8. The merits of this case are further developed by John Benson in the same volume of *The Testimony*, pages 305,6 and also by Barbara Spencer in *The Testimony*, Volume 68 (1998), pages 11-13.

12 – F. W. Farrar, *St. Luke – Cambridge Bible for Schools and Colleges*, page 372.

13 – Alfred Edersheim, *The Life and Times of Jesus the Messiah*, page 72.

14 – Frank Jannaway, *Christadelphian Answers*, page 20.

Elizabeth Evans[15] who draws attention to the prominence of female names in the Matthew genealogy and suggests this would be especially appropriate if the line comes down to Mary. Harry Whittaker offers yet another alternative. He suggests that the two genealogies may actually be of both Mary *and* Joseph, which would mean that Mary and Joseph were cousins.[16] Ever since ancient times it has been widely believed that Mary and Joseph were closely related.

Each of these views has passionate supporters: there is a detailed critique of the merits of several of these theories in *The Testimony* for 1942.[17] Those who might wish for a definitive and incontrovertible answer on the question of the Lord's genealogy must go away disappointed. What is beyond dispute, however, is that Mary must be descended from David for Jesus to have been "great David's greater son". The language of Luke 1:27,32 and 69 and Luke 2:4 make this abundantly clear. The testimony of the apostles (Romans 1:3; 2 Timothy 2:8 and Hebrews 7:14) also demands that Mary be descended from David.

Some commentators have questioned whether rights in Israel could pass through the female line. Jewish sceptics of the Messiahship of Jesus have used this to undermine his claim to the throne of his father David. In answer to a question from a reader in 1872 Robert Roberts addressed this issue and pointed out that within the tribe of Judah there is the case of the house of Sheshan being recognised, even though he had no sons and only daughters (1 Chronicles 2:31,34).[18] Thus descent through a female need not disqualify a man from his rightful inheritance.

That Mary was related to the tribe of Levi in some way is implied by her kinship with Elizabeth, the wife of Zacharias. This may have been possible (as suggested

---

15 – *The Testimony*, Volume 73 (2003), pages 224,225.
16 – Harry Whittaker, *Studies in the Gospels*, page 5.
17 – *The Testimony*, Volume 12 (1942), pages 213 to 216.
18 – *The Christadelphian*, Volume 9 (1872), page 40.

earlier) if Zacharias married a woman of Judah after the pattern of his ancestor Aaron. Another theory has been proposed by John Thomas in the following terms:

"Heli [in his view the father of Mary] married the sister of the father of Elizabeth, the wife of Zechariah, and mother of John the Baptizer, who was, therefore, second cousin to Jesus. Elizabeth was of the daughters of Aaron; consequently Mary, daughter of Heli and mother of Jesus, was of the house of David by her father, and of the house of Aaron by her mother: so that in her son Jesus was not only vested by his birth, and the marriage of his mother, all kingly rights, but all rego-pontifical as well. In Jesus, therefore, is united the combined kingly and high-priestly offices of the nation of Israel: so that when the government shall be upon his shoulders he will sit as a priest upon his throne, after the order of Melchizedek, being without predecessor or successor in the united office of king and priest."[19]

This is an attractive proposition, but unfortunately John Thomas does not provide any evidence for his assertion that Elizabeth's father was the sister of Mary's mother. The view that Mary was related through her mother to the tribe of Levi is, however, supported by Edersheim[20], who goes on to point out that this suggests that Mary came from a high-ranking family. As a descendant of David, Mary's family could be so described, although by the time Mary reached adulthood at least her branch of the family had become impoverished, perhaps through the early demise of her parents. That Mary may have had family connections with a priestly family is also suggested by the fact that the Apostle John, a cousin of Jesus, was "known to the high priest", as stated twice in John 18:15,16.

---

19 – John Thomas, *Herald of the Future Age*, Volume 3, page 34 (January, 1847).
20 – Alfred Edersheim, *The Life and Times of Jesus the Messiah*, page 72.

3

JOSEPH

"... a just man ..." (Matthew 1:19)

IT is implicit in Luke 1:34 that Mary's betrothed husband Joseph was an entirely honourable and upright man: "Mary said to the angel, 'How can this be, since I do not know a man?'" This would not have been true of all unmarried girls in Galilean villages, especially those as vulnerable as Mary. In seeking to develop an appreciation of Mary we do well to consider also the character of the man God providentially provided as her husband and as the foster father of His own Son.

In Matthew 1, Joseph, like Mary in Luke 1, receives a divine message from an angel. If Mary was the subject of lewd gossip in Nazareth we must assume that Joseph, as the man to whom she was betrothed, was also the victim of malicious comments. As in Mary's case, Joseph's personal integrity would only add to the anguish he felt.

Mary might have explained to Joseph what Gabriel had said, but the record appears to suggest that she did not. Possibly Mary assumed that Joseph would not believe her; who could be surprised that Joseph would struggle with such an explanation?

"Now the birth of Jesus Christ was as follows: after his mother Mary was betrothed to Joseph, before they came together, she was found with child of the Holy Spirit. Then Joseph her husband, being a just man, and not wanting to make her a public example, was minded to put her away secretly."

(Matthew 1:18,19)

17

It would seem that at the very least Mary did not immediately tell Joseph about her pregnancy; it was when Mary's condition became known that he considered putting her away.

It is possible that Mary went to see Elizabeth as soon as possible after her encounter with Gabriel and stayed three months with her cousin in Judea. She seems to have returned to "her house" at Nazareth three months into the pregnancy, after Elizabeth had given birth to John the Baptist, and of course the secret could not be concealed for much longer.

A just man

We can well understand how shocked and distressed Joseph would have been to learn that his fiancée had returned from a lengthy absence expecting a baby that was not his. Those fanciful gossips who took his side would have spun lurid tales to explain the pregnancy. It is clear that Joseph was an extraordinary Israelite, which might explain how he and Mary came to be engaged to one another, for he decided that he would not make a public example of his apparently unfaithful betrothed. Schonfield translates the phrase, "put her away secretly", as, "divorce her quietly", while Weymouth offers, "release her privately from the betrothal".

Verse 19 refers to Joseph as Mary's husband. Under Jewish custom a betrothed couple were regarded as husband and wife, but they could not have conjugal relations until the marriage itself. Betrothal for virgins lasted at least twelve months and was taken very seriously; it could be dissolved only by death or by a formal bill of divorce.[21] Under the Law of Moses the penalty for unfaithfulness on the part of a betrothed woman was stoning:

---

21 – *The Jewish Encyclopedia*, Volume VIII, page 349, Article Marriage Laws, Funk & Wagnalls, 1916; see also John Mitchell, The Pilgrimage of Jesus (2), *The Testimony*, Volume 26 (April 1956), page 110.

"If a young woman who is a virgin is betrothed to a husband, and a man finds her in the city and lies with her, then you shall bring them both out to the gate of that city, and you shall stone them to death with stones, the young woman because she did not cry out in the city, and the man because he humbled his neighbour's wife."   (Deuteronomy 22:23,24)

There is some doubt as to whether such a penalty was enforced in the days of Mary. Under the Romans the Jews lacked the authority to put someone to death (see John 18:31), but that did not stop them trying. There was more than one attempt to stone Jesus and they were successful in their stoning of Stephen in Acts 7. Regardless of whether the full penalty of the law could be implemented, we can appreciate the seriousness with which Joseph would have regarded this apparent breach of trust. A betrothed woman who was unfaithful was treated as an adulteress. It says much for his personal integrity and his high regard for Mary that he decided to act graciously by not making a public example of her. He retained a loving feeling for this young woman in spite of how she appeared to have betrayed him. This is an exhortation to all saints who would aspire to be 'just men'; we must never rush to condemn and we need to forgive as we would that God would forgive us.

It has been suggested[22] that the "evidence" of Mary's virginity (Deuteronomy 22:15) could be produced to confirm her virginity in spite of the fact that she was pregnant. If that were so it would only intensify the depth of Joseph's quandary as he wrestled with contradictory evidence about his fiancée.

A divine messenger reassured Joseph about the integrity of his wife-to-be:

---

22 – Colin Attridge, *Think on These Things*, pages 107-8. This view would not be sustainable if the tokens of a woman's virginity were (as most commentators claim) the bloodstained bed linen of the wedding night.

"But while he thought about these things, behold, the angel of the Lord appeared to him in a dream, saying, 'Joseph, son of David, do not be afraid to take to you Mary your wife, for that which is conceived in her is of the Holy Spirit. And she will bring forth a son, and you shall call his name JESUS, for he will save his people from their sins.'" (Matthew 1:20,21) This record certainly implies that, as suggested previously, Mary did not tell Joseph what Gabriel had said to her. If she did, it would appear Joseph did not believe her. The word Matthew uses to describe Joseph's thought processes speaks of mental anguish and carries the idea of turning things over in the mind due to commotion (the same word is used of Peter's mental turmoil when presented with the vision of the unclean animals in Acts 10:19). Joseph was greatly agitated by these developments. The angel's reassurance, therefore, was vital to restore his faith in Mary. It is much to his credit that Joseph accepted this remarkable revelation at face value. The angel knew Joseph would not doubt the message and in verse 21 his role as Mary's husband, and head of the household in which Jesus would be brought up, is assumed in that he is described as the one who would name the baby Jesus.

The angel refers to Joseph as "son of David". Regardless of how we read the genealogies in Matthew 1 and Luke 3, Joseph was a descendant of David. It seems unlikely, however, that this is the reason the angel used the messianic title, "son of David", to describe him. By this time David's descendants must have numbered in the thousands, yet this title is not used generally of those many male descendants. Of the sixteen times the term "son of David" is used in the New Testament, fourteen apply to the Lord Jesus Christ; apart from Joseph, the only other man so described is Nathan, David's literal son (in Luke 3:31). It would appear that the angel is linking Joseph to the messianic work of the boy of which he would be the guardian.

Matthew 1:22,23 almost certainly are words of Matthew explaining the significance of these things rather than a continuation of the angel's message:

"So all this was done that it might be fulfilled which was spoken by the Lord through the prophet, saying: 'Behold, the virgin shall be with child, and bear a Son, and they shall call his name Immanuel,' which is translated, 'God with us'".

In verse 24 Joseph acted promptly in taking Mary as his wife:

"Then Joseph, being raised from sleep, did as the angel of the Lord commanded him and took to him his wife."

One writer has commented on Joseph's prompt response: "In this experience of Joseph is exemplified the power of Christ (even before he was born) to win men from doubt to faith".[23] Joseph had been slow to condemn Mary and had agonized over what to do in response, but when he receives a divine command he is quick to obey. We see exactly the same alacrity to obey a further angelic command to take Mary and Jesus from Bethlehem to Egypt to avoid the evil intent of Herod (Matthew 2:13,14). In this regard also, Joseph is an exhortation to all who would be just.

It is appropriate to consider the magnitude of what Joseph was asked to undertake. As a faithful Jew he must have been among those yearning for the coming of Messiah. Now he is asked to take on the task of being foster father to Messiah – in its own way a task just as challenging as Mary's as the maidservant of the Lord. It must have been with a mixture of anxiety, awe, humility and wonder that Joseph contemplated this great responsibility. His wife pondered these things deeply and no doubt Joseph did likewise.

Joseph's marrying Mary immediately would have given her a measure of protection from the gossipmongers, but it would have done little to enhance

23 – Harry Whittaker, *Studies in the Gospels*, page 24.

his own standing in that close community. We may be certain that he remained the victim of innuendo. Joseph's gracious act would be interpreted as evidence of guilt. 'Who would do such a thing for a woman carrying another man's child?', we can hear these people asking, perhaps emboldened by a misapplication of the law which required a man who raped an unbetrothed girl to marry her (Deuteronomy 22:28,29), ignoring the fact that they were already betrothed. God's providence is evident in His selection of both Mary *and* Joseph – he was the right man for a very special task.

Through God's providence, this humble man would now provide a home and support for Mary during those daunting last days of her confinement. Their home would be a sanctuary where they could talk about the demands Mary would face as the mother and he would face as the foster father of the Messiah.

A carpenter

Joseph was a carpenter. The word means 'a worker in wood, a carpenter, joiner, builder' (Liddell and Scott). In a rural village in Galilee it is likely that the demand for a carpenter's skills would be limited to very basic needs. The inhabitants of Nazareth, including Mary and Joseph, lived in humble stone dwellings that the men of the family and their friends built and maintained. All the local men would have some level of expertise in basic construction skills; it is unlikely that a professional builder could have sustained himself in Nazareth.

While they would have almost no need for a builder, in their daily lives as subsistence farmers the residents of a Galilean village would require the assistance of skilled tradesmen such as ploughwrights to make and repair agricultural implements, and cabinet makers for the very few more elaborate items of furniture they used. This is consistent with an ancient tradition preserved by Justin Martyr, who wrote in about AD 150, that Jesus "was in the habit of working as a carpenter when among men, making ploughs and yokes" (*Dialogue with Trypho*, chapter 88).

Timber was relatively scarce in Israel by this time, although Galilee was more heavily timbered than most parts of the land, and it would appear that few men were skilled in working with wood. This is supported by the fact that, with the exception of Joseph, Jesus and Bezaleel (Exodus 31:2-5), in every instance in scripture where the origin of a carpenter is indicated he is identified as a foreigner: for example, carpenters from Tyre were responsible for the joinery in David's palace (2 Samuel 5:11) and Solomon's temple (1 Kings 5:18).

The Jews valued and respected trade skills but outside of the villages there seems to have been little demand for carpenters, while within the villages the demand would have been mainly related to agricultural tools crafted from wood. We may conclude, therefore, that it is most likely Joseph's trade, and that of Jesus in his turn, involved the manufacture and repair of wooden implements.

An old man?

It is frequently suggested that Joseph was much older than Mary and that this accounts for why he disappears (presumably due to death) from the record sometime after Jesus turned 12. There is absolutely no biblical support for this theory. The genesis of this idea probably was a desire to attribute the brothers and sisters of Jesus as the children of Joseph by a previous marriage. One ancient apocryphal work, *The Death of Joseph*, presents Joseph as having married his first wife at the age of 49 and being married to her for 40 years until she died. After a year of widowhood he is said to have been given to Mary when he was 90 and she was twelve or fourteen[24].

Unsubstantiated theories such as these have been exploited by the Roman Catholic Church to support its teaching that Mary remained a virgin all her life. Such

---

24 – Quoted in *Hasting's Bible Dictionary*, Volume 2, page 776.

a teaching is unnecessary and disrespectful, and in any event goes against the obvious implications of Matthew 1:25 in relation to Mary and Joseph.

Contrary to these apocryphal theories and in the absence of any evidence to the contrary we may assume that, consistent with Jewish custom at the time, Joseph was in his late teens or twenty at most when he married Mary. It would not be unusual that he died by his late thirties as the life expectancy of poor, labouring men was relatively short in the first century.

4

HIGHLY FAVOURED HANDMAID

"... save the son of your maidservant ..."
(Psalm 86:16)

CONSIDERABLE tension and pressure was borne by a humble, poor teenager – in the initial stage entirely alone. We sense in the record her shock and wonder, and not surprisingly she is perplexed by Gabriel's message:

"And having come in, the angel said to her, 'Rejoice, highly favoured one, the Lord is with you; blessed are you among women!' But when she saw him, she was troubled at his saying, and considered what manner of greeting this was." (Luke 1:28,29)

Such lofty language for a poor Galilean girl! Mary is to be "highly favoured" ("graciously accepted, or, much graced", AV margin; "endued with grace", RV margin; J. B. Phillips and the RSV render this phrase as, "O favoured one"). The word in Greek is *karito*, which Thayer says means, 'compass with favour'. This word appears only twice in scripture. The other use is in Ephesians 1:6 where it is translated as "accepted" and used of the graciousness extended to the saints through Christ:

"To the praise of the glory of his grace, by which he has made us accepted (Weymouth, 'enriched') in the Beloved".

Why was Mary compassed with favour by God? The phrase suggests that of all the teenage girls in Jewry God chose this particular one. Why? We cannot be dogmatic, but perhaps it reflects the deep spirituality she had developed at an early age. George Booker

25

makes an intriguing speculation that it may have been because she was in the habit of praying to play a part in the provision of Israel's Messiah.[25] The phrase, "Blessed are you among women", may not be in the original text of verse 28 (see RV, NIV, etc.), although in any event it appears again in verse 42.

Greatly troubled

In verse 29 the words of Gabriel trouble Mary: she "*considered* what manner of greeting this was". The Greek word, *diataratto*, is used only in this verse. Thayer says it means 'to agitate greatly'. The RSV and NIV say she was "greatly troubled", while the NEB has "deeply troubled". Why wouldn't she be? That she was the recipient of some special message was obvious, but what could it mean?

In verses 30-33 Gabriel explains his amazing message:

"Then the angel said to her, 'Do not be afraid, Mary, for you have found favour with God. And, behold, you will conceive in your womb and bring forth a son, and shall call his name JESUS. He will be great, and will be called the Son of the Highest; and the Lord God will give him the throne of his father David. And he will reign over the house of Jacob forever; and of his kingdom there will be no end'."

We know these words so well, but how must they have hit this poor teenager! Elements of the message would have made sense because the Jews expected that one day their Messiah would be born in a Jewish family, but the full import could hardly have been completely appreciated. Yet Mary's calmness is simply astounding when she meekly asks in verse 34 how this could be possible given that she is a virgin. She does not doubt that Messiah would come as the angel said, but surely his mother would need to be married.

Mary's meek question, "How can this be, since I do not know a man?", expressed entirely reasonable

---

25 – G. Booker, *Unto Us a Child is Born ...*, page 12.

bewilderment, not a lack of faith or sense of incredulity. Her question stands in stark contrast, therefore, with Zacharias' question to the angel in verse 18 when he expressed doubt that the thing promised could be possible given his own physical limitations and those of Elizabeth. Mary never doubted that with God all things are possible. In their contrasting responses to the angel, Zacharias and Mary embodied the difference between the dispensations of law and grace to which they stood related.

Verses 30-33, remarkable though they are, contain ideas which devout Israelites could understand to a certain degree. The words that follow in verses 35-37, however, are much more remarkable:

"The angel answered and said to her, 'The Holy Spirit will come upon you, and the power of the Highest will overshadow you; therefore, also, that holy one who is to be born will be called the Son of God. Now indeed, Elizabeth your relation has also conceived a son in her old age; and this is now the sixth month with her who was called barren. For with God nothing will be impossible'."

Even today, with the benefit of hindsight and a complete scripture record, the message of verse 35 defies our comprehension. The angel's final words in verse 37 are an understatement in the circumstances. With God nothing shall be impossible – for the barren Elizabeth as well as for the virgin Mary! Those words must have resonated in Mary's devout mind for years to come, and in Elizabeth's mind too, for we may be certain that Mary related them to her when she went to stay with her.

The phrase the angel uttered ("with God nothing will be impossible") was a clear allusion to the angel's statement to Sarah in Genesis 18:14. Sarah had doubted (arguably with good reason!) the angel's prediction that she would have a son. Mary, however, never doubted. There is a world of difference between bewilderment and doubt.

27

God's handmaid

Verse 35 has overtones of Genesis 1 and the natural creation, where the spirit of God is presented as moving over the face of the waters. Gabriel, who witnessed that creation, was describing the genesis of the new creation, the most amazing development in the world since creation itself. Mary is told she will be at the very heart of these stupendous developments. In spite of the momentous nature of the message Mary accepted the challenges before her, as her response in verse 38 shows: "Behold the maidservant of the Lord! Let it be to me according to your word".

Not all women would have been so accepting in these circumstances. Some may have said something like 'Why me?' or 'I still do not understand how all this will happen'. Not Mary! There must have been a hundred questions, myriad uncertainties and countless apprehensions, yet Mary accepted her role as God's maidservant. This reflects the meek and compliant spirit of a faithful young woman in Israel, but the magnitude of what she was being asked to do must have been more daunting than the challenges other teenagers in rural Galilee would be expected to handle.

The Greek word for maidservant is *doulee*, a female slave or servant, especially one who renders involuntary service. It is used only three times in scripture – twice of Mary (here and in verse 48), and once in Acts 2:18.

The use of this word testifies to Mary's remarkable spirituality even at that young age. It would seem that upon hearing Gabriel's explanation that the child she would carry would be the Son of God, Mary's thoughts went straight to two messianic Psalms where the Messiah is spoken of as the Son of God's maidservant.

Psalm 86 presents to us a Messiah who is poor and needy, just as the son of Mary and Joseph would have been. Throughout Psalm 86 there are images of the salvation God offers through Messiah. Towards the end of the Psalm there is also a clear allusion to the

28

opposition our Lord would face from the Jewish leaders: "O God, the proud have risen against me, and a mob of violent men have sought my life, and have not set you before them" (verse 14). The Psalmist then goes on to speak of the need to save "the son of your maidservant". "Oh, turn to me, and have mercy upon me! Give your strength to your servant, and save the son of your maidservant" (verse 16).

Mary's identification of herself as the maidservant of the Lord suggests that she understood the messianic significance of this Psalm. That being so, what did she make of the clear overtones of hostility towards the Messiah of which the Psalm speaks? The positive and negative aspects of the Psalm must have formed part of her ponderings for many years.

Psalm 116 is another unmistakably messianic Psalm, crammed with allusions to the death and resurrection of the Messiah. As a Psalm sung on Passover night and several other occasions through the year, Mary would have been very familiar with its words. Curiously she would have sung these words each year in Jerusalem for she travelled there annually to celebrate Passover (Luke 2:41) and it was in that city that some of the most foreboding words of the Psalm would be realised. In verse 16 the Messiah is described as "the son of your maidservant": "O LORD, truly I am your servant; I am your servant, the son of your maidservant; you have loosed my bonds." As Mary identified herself to Gabriel as the Lord's maidservant she may have been conscious of the heavy message embodied in this Psalm about the death of her son. Throughout Psalm 116 there are references to his death – for example in verses 3 and 4, verse 8 and in particular in verse 15: "Precious in the sight of the LORD is the death of his saints."

We may be confident that during the nine months between the visit of Gabriel and the birth of Jesus Mary's thoughts turned time and again to these Psalms, at times with joyous anticipation and at other times with foreboding. Forty days after the Lord was born they must have flooded back into her mind when they went up to the temple for purification and encountered Simeon. His words picked up the twin themes of these Psalms – the promise of deliverance yet the persecution of the one who would bring deliverance:

"'Lord, now you are letting your servant depart in peace, according to your word; for my eyes have seen your salvation which you have prepared before the face of all peoples, a light to bring revelation to the Gentiles, and the glory of your people Israel.' And Joseph and his mother marvelled at those things which were spoken of him. Then Simeon blessed them, and said to Mary his mother, 'Behold, this child is destined for the fall and rising of many in Israel, and for a sign which will be spoken against (yes, a sword will pierce through your own soul also), that the thoughts of many hearts may be revealed'."

(Luke 2:29-35)

Simeon's comments encapsulate the ministry of our Lord – the true Messiah and yet one who would face opposition from within the nation. And in verse 35 Simeon makes the point that the Lord's sufferings would have a profound impact on Mary personally. Think what it would mean for a teenage mother to receive such a dramatic message, especially after ten months of emotional turmoil – the most difficult ten months she would have experienced in her short life. Her highly developed appreciation of spiritual matters would prove to be both a blessing and a burden: a blessing as she saw God's plan for redemption being worked out; and a burden as she came to understand the agonising cost for herself and her son.

In Luke 1:38, the second half of Mary's response to the angel is highly significant given the insights suggested by the use of the word maidservant: "Be it to me according to your word." This was not a throwaway line. Her quiet resignation to God's will is made in the knowledge (imperfect no doubt, but clear enough) of what being God's maidservant would mean for her son

30

and for herself. It was an intelligent response based on an understanding of the word of God – both the words that the angel had just spoken and the written word of God in the Old Testament.

The solemn words of Psalm 116 in particular would recur as a refrain throughout her life. This Psalm is part of the Egyptian Hallel (Psalms 113 to 118). They were sung by the Jews every Passover night. We know that Mary placed a high importance on observance of the Passover for it is recorded that Mary and Joseph "went to Jerusalem every year at the Feast of the Passover" (Luke 2:41). Every year in Jerusalem she would hear this Psalm. Every year she would be reminded of her role as God's maidservant, and of the implications for her son – implications that would be worked out in the very city she was visiting.

To Elizabeth

Gabriel's message must have filled Mary with mixed feelings. One author has speculated about her emotional state in the months following Gabriel's visit:

"The months that followed would contain some of the sweetest moments of Mary's life; wonderment, expectation and exquisite joy, mingled with the fear of the unknown; in fact, all the emotions of expectant motherhood would be hers, and intensified a hundredfold by the knowledge of her wonderful secret. But even in those early days there were shadows; things she could not understand; things which frightened her."[26]

In the circumstances it is hardly surprising that an orphan girl would wish to spend time with someone sympathetic.

In Luke 1:34 Mary was mystified as to how she could bear a son when she was a virgin. Gabriel explained in verse 35 that the Holy Spirit would overshadow Mary and through that means the child would be conceived. Mary could not be expected to understand exactly how

26 – Lilian Adams, *The Testimony*, Volume 10 (1940), page 96.

this could be so any more than we can understand it. Gabriel recognised that this information would be hard to accept, and in verse 36 informed Mary of another miraculous event which would help to bolster her confidence in what she had been told:

> "Now indeed, Elizabeth your relation has also conceived a son in her old age; and this is now the sixth month for her, who was called barren."

Evidently the fact that her kinswoman Elizabeth had by a divine miracle conceived a child was intended to provide Mary with a degree of certainty about her own situation. It is also likely that Gabriel was hinting that Mary should go to Elizabeth, perhaps as a place of refuge, and it seems that as soon as the angel left Mary at the end of verse 38 she acted on that hint and departed Nazareth to spend time with Elizabeth. She shared her news with Elizabeth. If there was anyone in Israel who would be able to appreciate its significance it would have been the woman who was to be the mother of John the Baptist.

Where did Elizabeth live? Presumably she resided in one of the priestly cities. The record says she lived in the hill country of Judea, the elevated area surrounding Jerusalem. It has been suggested that Zacharias and Elizabeth lived in Hebron, a Levitical city about 20 miles south of Jerusalem. It may seem appropriate that Mary should go to a city of refuge for comfort and support. It may also seem appropriate that the mother of David's greatest son should find a haven in the city where David had been anointed king over Israel.

If Hebron was the home town of Elizabeth, Mary's journey must have taken her via Jerusalem. Given her highly developed spirituality she would have had much to contemplate as she passed through the Holy City. It would have been an obvious place to break her journey and spend a night before moving on to Hebron. What thoughts might have filled her head as she lay down to rest in the city of David! This was the city where the throne her son was to inherit had been established.

This was also the city where the last king to occupy that throne, Zedekiah, had been dethroned in accordance with Ezekiel's words: "Overthrown, overthrown, I will make it overthrown! It shall be no longer, until he comes whose right it is, and I will give it to him" (Ezekiel 21:27). In her womb was the one "whose right it is".

A different tradition from the sixth century suggests that Elizabeth lived in Ain Karim, a village five miles from Jerusalem, while some commentators have suggested Juttah, also a town allocated to Judah (Joshua 15:55). We cannot be dogmatic about where Elizabeth lived. What is clear is that the site was well south of Nazareth and would have involved a solitary journey of several days over up to 100 miles for a somewhat amazed and rather friendless young woman. Even if there were others on the road as Mary travelled, we might expect her to feel somewhat isolated because she would be unable to speak very openly about her circumstances. That Mary undertook such a journey is testimony both to the enormity of the challenge she faced and to the courage and determination she possessed.

Elizabeth was a Levite, but she was not just from any Levitical family; she is specifically identified as being "of the daughters of Aaron" (Luke 1:5). Her name is equivalent to the Hebrew Elisheba, a name she shared with the wife of her great ancestor Aaron (Exodus 6:23). Curiously, Elisheba was of the tribe of Judah, a tribe to which her latter-day namesake was also related. In Mary (Miriam) and Elizabeth (Elisheba) we have names which link the events of Luke 1 directly with the establishment of the Mosaic order in Exodus. Mary and her cousin were clearly chosen to usher in a new dispensation which would fulfil and build upon the Law of Moses.

The response of Elizabeth to the astonishing news Mary brought was guileless and faithful:

"Blessed are you among women, and blessed is the fruit of your womb! But why is this granted to me, that the mother of my Lord should come to me? For indeed, as soon as the voice of your greeting sounded in my ears, the babe leaped in my womb for joy. Blessed is she who believed, for there will be a fulfilment of those things which were told her from the Lord." (Luke 1:42-45) Mary found that what Gabriel had told her about Elizabeth was true. This must have had a profound impact on Mary. "Not only did Mary find that it was perfectly true that Elizabeth was having a child in her old age, but as soon as she entered the house Elizabeth confirmed the annunciation by greeting Mary by inspiration as the mother of the Messiah. How happy Mary would be to have this double supernatural affirmation of the things the angel had told her!"[27]

Elizabeth speaks of Mary as being "blessed ... among women". In Judges 5:24, in the Song of Deborah, Jael was described in similar language for her role in slaying Sisera. This was a type of the conquest of the power of sin – the bruising of the head of the serpent. And now the language was applied to the mother of the one who would fulfil that type.

There is a remarkable emphasis on females in the story of Deborah. Deborah herself drew attention to the leadership vacuum in Israel which required "a mother in Israel" (Judges 5:7) to step into the breach. Jael plays a key role in killing Sisera (Judges 4:21), and Sisera's mother drew attention to the way in which the Canaanites oppressed the Israelite women (Judges 5:30). Just as Jael "bruised" Israel's oppressor by delivering a fatal wound to the head, so Mary's child would fulfil the promise to Eve in Genesis 3:15. This realisation must be behind Elizabeth's exclamation to Mary: "Blessed is the fruit of your womb" – she

---

27 – Peggy Price, *Women of the Bible*, "Mary, the Mother of Jesus", page 170.

recognised this child Mary was carrying as the promised seed of the woman.

As in the days of Deborah, in Mary's time there was a leadership vacuum in Israel, with the religious rulers being described as "blind leaders of the blind" (Matthew 15:14, and see also Matthew 23:2,3). In spite of that fact, faithful women like Mary, Elizabeth, Anna, Mary and Martha of Bethany and so many others co-operate in the fulfilment of God's redemptive plan. The events concerning the conception and birth of Jesus as recorded in Luke place particular emphasis on women. It has been observed[28] that the book of Luke places a heavy emphasis generally on women, in particular unmarried women (including widows) and the childless.

In verse 45 Elizabeth commented on the faith of Mary: "Blessed is she who believed". These words might sound glib, but as we have seen the faith of Mary was truly amazing. What she heard must have taxed her in every way, yet she believed it all implicitly, such was the intense spirituality of this young teenager. And Mary would need a strong and robust faith to cope with what was to unfold. No doubt there were days when she would have echoed the words of another in the Gospel records: "Lord, I believe; help my unbelief" (Mark 9:24).

Elizabeth may well have been conscious of the necessity of such a strong faith in what had been revealed to Mary. Elizabeth would have been the focus of much rejoicing as her friends and relatives celebrated with her the unexpected blessing of a longed-for child. Her cousin would not be so fortunate. Mary for the rest of her life would be the subject of an unending stream of malicious gossip and innuendo about the child she had conceived in such miraculous circumstances.

Mary's willingness to believe stands in stark contrast to the incredulity of Elizabeth's husband Zacharias. When confronted by an angel (Gabriel?) he did not believe what he was told (Luke 1:20). As a consequence

---

28 – See Mary Benson, "The Women of Luke's Gospel", *The Testimony*, Volume 77, pages 264-268.

Zacharias was struck dumb. It was not until more than nine months later when his son was born that Zacharias was able to speak again, and on that occasion he uttered a great prophetic song. Mary, however, believed from the start, displaying a meek acceptance of the will of God and a humble determination to act in accordance with His will, whatever the cost.

Mary is an example to us all. The Song of Mary in Luke 1:46-55 is further evidence of Mary's highly developed spirituality, expressing through song a profound appreciation of the Old Testament promises and prophecies.

5

THE SONG OF MARY

"Oh, sing to the LORD a new song! For he has done marvellous things; his right hand and his holy arm have gained him the victory." (Psalm 98:1)

TEENAGERS are often very aware of spiritual matters. It is a time in life when men and women are often very much in touch with their emotions and think deeply about the things of life. This is especially true of teenagers who grow up in a society where children take on the challenges of adulthood at an early age and for children such as orphans whose family circumstances have been disrupted. Even within such a framework the spirituality of the teenage Mary was remarkable. This is evident from her first encounter with Gabriel. Her response to the angel's astounding message was so meek and composed because her mind went immediately to the promise to David and to the messianic prophecies in the Psalms. The Song of Mary in Luke 1:46 to 55 is further evidence of Mary's highly developed appreciation of the Old Testament promises and prophecies:

"My soul magnifies the Lord, and my spirit has rejoiced in God my Saviour. For he has regarded the lowly state of his maidservant; for behold, henceforth all generations will call me blessed. For he who is mighty has done great things for me, and holy is his name. And his mercy is on those who fear him from generation to generation. He has shown strength with his arm; he has scattered the proud in the imagination of their hearts. He has put down the mighty from their thrones, and exalted the lowly. He has filled the hungry with good things, and the rich he has sent away empty. He has helped his servant

MARY: HANDMAID OF THE LORD

Israel, in remembrance of his mercy, as he spoke to our fathers, to Abraham and to his seed for ever."

The Song of Mary has been described as "a mosaic of quotations from the Old Testament".[29] In her song Mary quotes from nine separate books of scripture and in particular draws heavily on Hannah's song in 1 Samuel 2. Of course there are several parallels between these two women (these are discussed in the next chapter).

We marvel at the depth of understanding of this Jewish teenager, and also at her astonishing courage, composure and commitment. This is an inspiration and a challenge to all the faithful, and to the young in particular. Are we as dedicated and committed as this young woman? Have we applied ourselves to the scriptures, as Mary obviously had, to develop a keen appreciation of God's plan of salvation? No wonder the record in Luke 1 describes her as "blessed".

At the conclusion of the last chapter we left Mary in Judea with her cousin. Elizabeth was also the subject of miraculous intervention by God, yet she readily recognised that Mary's situation was vastly different. Both women recognised the momentous nature of what was happening to Mary and shared in the excitement. Mary responded to Elizabeth's outburst with the stirring song recorded by Luke. Its opening words express so much about Mary's character – "My soul magnifies the Lord". With her whole body, both figuratively and in a unique sense literally, Mary magnified or extolled the Lord.

Psalm 34 – magnify the LORD
Almost certainly this thought is drawn from Psalm 34 where David extolled God for His overshadowing protection. Mary would feel in need of this as she went forth as the Lord's handmaid. The language of the Psalm suggests that Mary chose this allusion to Psalm 34 as a means of including Elizabeth in her praise. Note

---

29 – F. W. Farrar, St. Luke (*Cambridge Bible for Schools and Colleges*), page 55.

the plural element in verses 2 and 3 – "with me", "us" and "together":

"My soul shall make its boast in the LORD; the humble shall hear of it and be glad. Oh magnify the LORD *with me*, and let *us* exalt his name *together*."

We can see the links with Mary's words. And as the Psalm develops we can see how much comfort Mary would have drawn as she contemplated its words at this time. In verses 4 to 6 there is much to which Mary could relate as she contemplated returning to her home in Nazareth:

"I sought the LORD, and he heard me, and delivered me from all my fears. They looked to him and were radiant, and their faces were not ashamed. This poor man cried out, and the LORD heard him, and saved him out of all his troubles."

Fear, shame, poverty and trouble – all of these were to be Mary's lot in the next nine months, and throughout her life. What profound strength she must have found, then, in some of the later verses in Psalm 34:

"The angel of the LORD encamps all around those that fear him, and delivers them." (verse 7)

"Many are the afflictions of the righteous, but the LORD delivers him out of them all." (verse 19)

Afflictions aplenty would come upon Mary, as they do on so many of the faithful, but Mary and those who share her faith may draw comfort from the certainty that the God of Israel encamps about them and will deliver them. And for Mary the thought of divine deliverance must inevitably have involved contemplation of the child she was to bear as the maidservant of the Lord.

God my Saviour

We can now appreciate a little more the thoughts that brought forth this song. And it was not just her natural self that magnified the Lord. In Luke 1:47 her spirit also is engaged: "My spirit has rejoiced in God my Saviour."

39

From verse 47 the song is expressed in the past tense. Mary's profound faith was such that God's purpose had already been accomplished. The reference to "spirit" in verse 47 might indicate that she was aware that her words were inspired by God, or it might refer to her character. Whichever it is, Mary rejoiced in "God her saviour". This title is an allusion to the name "Jesus" that the angel Gabriel told her she would give her son – "Jesus" means 'Yahweh shall save'. God as saviour is a theme in many prophetic books, especially in Isaiah (e.g., Isaiah 43:11; 45:21 and 49:26). In Habakkuk the concept of God as a saviour is firmly rooted in a messianic prophecy that may have had a special force for Mary:

"Though the fig tree may not blossom, nor fruit be on the vines; though the labour of the olive may fail, and the fields yield no food; though the flock may be cut off from the fold, and there be no herd in the stalls – yet I will rejoice in the LORD, I will joy in the God of my salvation." (Habakkuk 3:17,18)

Given the trials that were ahead these words must have resonated with Mary.

In the New Testament the concepts of God as our saviour and of the Lord Jesus Christ as saviour become interchangeable. Mary was central to this development. Paul takes up both concepts in consecutive verses in a remarkable passage:

"But (God) has in due time manifested his word through preaching, which was committed to me according to the commandment of *God our Saviour*; to Titus, a true son in our common faith: grace, mercy, and peace from God the Father and the *Lord Jesus Christ our Saviour*." (Titus 1:3,4)

God's maidservant

Mary returns to her role as God's maidservant in Luke 1:48: "For He has regarded the lowly state of His maidservant; for behold, henceforth all generations will call me blessed".

We have already considered how the word "maidservant" is a link to Psalms 86 and 116. And indeed Mary's was a lowly state, as we have also considered. The word translated "lowly state" is the Greek *tapinosis*. Literally it means 'humiliation' and it is used only four times in scripture. The other three uses are interesting:

- Acts 8:33 – of the Lord Jesus Christ.
- Philippians 3:21 – of our human nature that needs to be changed by the Lord.
- James 1:10 – refers to a humiliation we must not shun as brothers and sisters of Christ. It speaks of the humiliation that we need to cultivate if we wish to be exalted in the age to come: "Let the lowly brother glory in his exaltation, but the rich in his humiliation, because as a flower of the field he will pass away" (James 1:9,10).

God raises the poor and humble, those with a contrite spirit like Mary, to heavenly places. Mary said in Luke 1:48 that "all generations will call me blessed". More than 2,000 years after this song was spoken we recognise her blessed role in God's redemptive plan. "Blessed" means 'happy'. In what sense do we regard Mary as happy? As we shall see, her life was one of great trouble and sorrow. The Greek word used by Mary is *makarizo*, which Bullinger defines as "to call happy". This word is used only twice in the New Testament and the other use is in James 5:11:

"My brethren, take the prophets, who spoke in the name of the Lord, as an example of suffering and patience. Indeed we count them blessed who endure. You have heard of the perseverance of Job and seen the end intended by the Lord – that the Lord is very compassionate and merciful."   (verses 10,11)

This is the sense in which Mary is called 'happy'. This happiness has nothing to do with an easy life, material contentment and superficial merriment. Like Job, Mary endured much heartache but she had confidence in

God's overshadowing care and was certain that God would deliver to the uttermost.

Psalm 126 – He is mighty

Mary goes on to speak of her direct involvement in God's plan:

> "For he who is mighty has done great things for me, and holy is his name." (verse 49)

"He who is mighty" has echoes of the angel's message in verse 35 that the "power of the highest" would come upon her. The Holy Spirit did come upon Mary and, as she said, He "has done great things for me". "He who is mighty" could also hark back to the angel Gabriel, whose name (according to Young's) may mean 'God is mighty',[30] who brought this news to Mary. While this may be true, the passage on which Mary's statement is based is probably Psalm 126, a Psalm which is so applicable to the situation in which she now found herself:

> "When the LORD brought back the captivity of Zion, we were like those that dream. Then our mouth was filled with laughter, and our tongue with singing. Then said they among the nations, 'The LORD has done great things for them.' The LORD has done great things for us, and we are glad." (Psalm 126:1-3)

This is the situation in which mankind was found when Gabriel came to Mary; in bondage to sin and death. And in verse 2 the Psalmist's realisation that God would intervene to overcome this bondage brings forth song as it did for Mary. Verses 2 and 3 both speak of God doing great things, and the remainder of the Psalm is especially applicable to Mary:

> "Bring back our captivity, O LORD, as the streams in the south. Those who sow in tears shall reap in joy. He who continually goes forth weeping, bearing seed for sowing, shall doubtless come again with rejoicing, bringing his sheaves with him." (Psalm 126:4-6)

---

30 – Some other authorities suggest that Gabriel means 'man of God'.

Mary was deeply conscious of the deliverance that was tied up in her work as the handmaid of God. There would be more than a few tears, as verse 5 suggests, but much joy in the end. And in verse 6 the one who weeps even though she carries the precious seed shall rejoice in the end.

Great mercy

In her song Mary declared the holiness of God's name and spoke of the wonder that, in spite of that holiness, God extends mercy to men and women:

"And his mercy is on those who fear him from generation to generation."   (verse 50)

The juxtaposition of the "name" in verse 49 and "mercy" in verse 50 reminds us that in Exodus 34:6,7 the very first divine characteristic associated with the revelation of the Memorial Name is that God is "merciful". Mary would have been conscious of this. She would also have been conscious of the message of the Psalmist in Psalm 103:

"He has not dealt with us according to our sins, nor punished us according to our iniquities. For as the heavens are high above the earth, so great is his mercy toward those who fear him."

(Psalm 103:10,11)

Mercy is extended, as Mary said, to those with a reverential fear of God. Later in Psalm 103 this concept is expanded with reference to the perpetuity of God's mercy:

"But the mercy of the LORD is from everlasting to everlasting on those who fear him, and his righteousness to children's children, to such as keep his covenant, and to those that remember his commandments to do them."   (Psalm 103:17,18)

Psalm 89 is another psalm that might well have been in Mary's mind at this time:

"I will sing of the mercies of the LORD forever: with my mouth will I make known your faithfulness to all generations. For I have said, 'Mercy shall be built up

43

forever; your faithfulness you shall establish in the very heavens.' I have made a covenant with my chosen, I have sworn to David my servant: 'Your seed will I establish forever, and build up your throne to all generations.'" (Psalm 89:1-4) The Psalm commences with a reference to God's perpetual mercy[31] in the context of the covenant with David (the promise to David must have been at the forefront of her mind in the days following the angel's remarkable statement to her in Luke 1:32). How powerful these words would have been to the young Mary as she contemplated her role as the handmaid of the Lord, chosen to bear the seed of David.

The arm of the Lord

Mary moved on in her song and made some very dramatic statements. She dwelt upon the militant power of Almighty God in verse 51: "He has shown strength with his arm; he has scattered the proud in the imagination of their hearts". The language in this short verse is amongst the richest in Old Testament allusions in a song heavy with such references.

Firstly, it seems certain that Mary must have been conscious of Psalm 98 at this point. Psalm 98 concerns a song about the wondrous doings of God and the revelation of His mighty arm:

"Oh, sing to the LORD a new song! For he has done marvellous things; his right hand and his holy arm have gained him the victory." (Psalm 98:1)

The themes of the Song of Mary pervade Psalm 98. Verse 2 refers to salvation, while verse 3 speaks of mercy, extended even to Gentiles as it is in Christ:

---

31 – The word translated "mercy" (Hebrew, *chesed*) is often used in association with the promises to Abraham and David. In addition to Psalm 89 the following examples are worth considering in this regard: Genesis 24:27; 32:19; Deuteronomy 7:9,12; 2 Samuel 7:15; 22:51; 1 Kings 8:23; 1 Chronicles 16:34,41; 17:13; Nehemiah 1:5; 9:32; Psalm 18:50; 98:3; 138:2,8; Isaiah 55:3; Lamentations 3:22,32; Daniel 9:4 and Micah 7:18-20.

'The LORD has made known his salvation; his righteousness he has revealed in the sight of the nations. He has remembered his mercy and his faithfulness to the house of Israel; all the ends of the earth have seen the salvation of our God."

(Psalm 98:2,3)

Well might those who rejoice in the wonder of this mercy sing and make a joyful noise!

The "arm of the Lord" is one of the great messianic themes of scripture.[32] An arm speaks of power and the wielding of that power to achieve an outcome. We can appreciate the imagery of God reaching out to save the perishing:

"Behold, the LORD's hand is not shortened, that it cannot save." (Isaiah 59:1)

The prophet's image is of a hand that is not closed in a fist but rather extended to offer a perishing man something onto which to grasp, as a man might reach from a boat in an attempt to pull a drowning man to safety. As Mary said, the arm which reaches out to perishing man is strong to save – strong because it is strengthened by God.

The arm that is mighty to save is also an instrument of judgement. We have already noticed that Psalm 89 has links to the Song of Mary. Verse 10 refers to the mighty arm of God in this context of judgement:

"You have broken Rahab in pieces, as one who is slain; you have scattered your enemies with your mighty arm." (Psalm 89:10)

In Psalm 89 it is the enemies of God who are scattered by God's mighty arm. In Mary's song it is the proud who are scattered. As we shall see, the proud were indeed the enemies of God, and we may be quite certain about exactly who these proud enemies were in the context of the life of Mary and her son.

---

32 – See, for instance, Psalm 44:3; 89:10,21; Isaiah 40:10,11; 51:5,9; 53:1; 59:16; 63:5; John 12:38.

Imagination of their hearts

Mary said that God had scattered "the proud in the imagination of their hearts". "The imagination of their hearts" is a phrase linked closely in scripture to sin and rebellion from its first dramatic use in Genesis 6:5. There is a sense, therefore, in which Mary's language speaks generically of the overthrow of sin. There is, however, a more direct and primary application of Mary's words.

Jeremiah used this phrase repeatedly and an analysis of those references identifies the class to whom Mary's words primarily relate:

• Jerusalem corrupted:

"At that time Jerusalem shall be called the Throne of the LORD, and all the nations shall be gathered to it, to the name of the LORD, to Jerusalem. No more shall they follow the dictates of their evil hearts."

(Jeremiah 3:17)

• The leaders corrupted:

"And the LORD said, 'Because they have forsaken my law which I set before them, and have not obeyed my voice, nor walked according to it, but they have walked according to the dictates of their own hearts and after the Baals, which their fathers taught them,' therefore thus says the LORD of hosts, the God of Israel: 'Behold, I will feed them, this people, with wormwood, and give them water of gall to drink. I will scatter them also among the Gentiles, whom neither they nor their fathers have known. And I will send a sword after them until I have consumed them.'" (9:13-16)

• The proud scattered:

"Thus says the LORD: 'In this manner I will ruin the pride of Judah and the great pride of Jerusalem. This evil people, who refuse to hear my words, who follow the dictates of their hearts, and walk after other gods to serve them and worship them, shall be

46

just like this sash which is profitable for nothing.'"
(13:9,10)

• Worse than their fathers:

"And you have done worse than your fathers, for behold, each one follows the dictates of his own evil heart, so that no one listens to me. Therefore I will cast you out of this land into a land that you do not know, neither you nor your fathers; and there you shall serve other gods day and night, where I will not show you favour." (16:12,13)

• Abandoned hope:

"And they said, 'That is hopeless! So we will walk according to our own plans, and we will every one do the imagination of his evil heart' ... 'I will scatter them as with an east wind before the enemy; I will show them the back and not the face in the day of their calamity.'" (18:12,17)

• Scattered by corrupt leaders:

"'Woe to the shepherds who destroy and scatter the sheep of my pasture!' says the LORD. Therefore thus says the LORD God of Israel against the shepherds who feed my people: 'You have scattered my flock, driven them away, and not attended to them. Behold, I will attend to you for the evil of your doings,' says the LORD ... They continually say to those who despise me, 'The LORD has said, "You shall have peace"'; and to everyone who walks according to the imagination of his own heart, they say, 'No evil shall come upon you.'" (23:1,2,17)

But the promise to David would be fulfilled regardless!

• A saviour raised up by God to overcome those who walk after the imagination of their heart:

"'Behold, the days are coming,' says the LORD, 'that I will raise to David a Branch of righteousness; a King shall reign and prosper, and execute judgment and righteousness in the earth. In his days Judah will be saved, and Israel will dwell safely; now this is

47

his name by which he shall be called: THE LORD OUR
RIGHTEOUSNESS.'" (23:5,6)

In Jeremiah 3:17 the prophet referred to the future
exaltation of Jerusalem and of the throne of David and
compared it with the corruption of earlier times. In
chapter 9:13-16 the prophet said that the Jewish
leadership had rejected him by walking after the
imagination of their hearts and that as a result he
would scatter them. In Jeremiah 13:9,10 it was again
the leaders who are targeted – the proud who Mary said
would be scattered, and the prophet had a similar
message in chapter 16:12,13. The same message is
found in Jeremiah 18:12 and 17.

In Jeremiah 23:1,2 the prophet said it was the
leaders who scatter Israel, because it is they who
provoke God to take that action. And how did they
provoke God so terribly? Verse 17 said it was by
walking according to the dictates of their own hearts!

It seems likely that Mary was conscious of all of this.
Her allusion to this theme in Jeremiah testifies that
she understood the intense conflict that would arise
between her son and the corrupt Jewish leaders. But
Mary, strengthened by the words of Gabriel, was
heartened by her understanding that her son would
fulfil the promise to David and deliver God's people, as
Jeremiah said in chapter 23:5,6.

Exalted the lowly

Building on these rich allusions Mary went on to say:
"He has put down the mighty from their thrones,
and exalted the lowly." (Luke 1:52)

As with some of the earlier themes, there was a general
sense in which this was to be fulfilled. In a direct sense,
however, Mary was referring primarily to the fact that
our Lord would overturn the Jewish order. Those
leaders who turned against him – the proud in the
terms of verse 51 – would in their turn be overthrown
by God, while the humble, those in a lowly state, the
humiliated, will be exalted in Christ.

48

In verse 48 Mary identified herself as one of "lowly state" (Greek, *tapinosis*). In verse 52 Mary used a closely related word, *tapinos*, to speak of a class which included her. That particular word is also used of her son in Matthew 11:29 ("I am meek and lowly in heart").

The saints must develop this same sense of lowliness, and they must, like Almighty God, reach out to those of low degree, in which spirit Paul exhorted the Romans, "Do not set your mind on high things, but associate with the humble" (Romans 12:16). Both James and Peter drew attention to God's graciousness towards the humble (James 4:6 and 1 Peter 5:5), on both occasions using the same Greek word Mary used in Luke 1:52.

Elsewhere the prophet Isaiah described both the majesty of the God of Israel and the condition of the people to whom He condescends:

"For thus says the High and Lofty One who inhabits eternity, whose name is Holy: 'I dwell in the high and holy place, with him who has a contrite and humble spirit, to revive the spirit of the humble, and to revive the heart of the contrite ones.'"

(Isaiah 57:15)

The great Creator of the universe condescends to men of low estate and gives grace to the humble. Unlike the rulers of Mary's time, such people have profound respect for the word of God:

"On this one will I look: on him who is poor and of a contrite spirit, and who trembles at my word."

(66:2)

Far from trembling at the word, the rulers at the time of Jesus would reject and murder the very one who was the word made flesh in an effort to preserve their own status – no contrition, no humility, no recognition of the supremacy of Almighty God from these men, just rank envy and hatred. Their days were numbered, however, when they turned against the Messiah, and in due course God would "exalt them of low degree". It is interesting that James would later write to Jewish believers, some of whom may have suffered at the hands of those who had persecuted their master, and exhort them to recognise the wonder of their position: "Let the lowly (*tapinos*) brother glory in his exaltation" (James 1:9), a truth to which Mary gave voice in her song.

The poor and hungry

In verse 53 Mary spoke of God filling the hungry and rejecting the rich: "He has filled the hungry with good things, and the rich he has sent away empty". This was in stark contrast with the behaviour of the Jewish leaders. They saw wealth as a token of God's evident blessing. Not so our Lord.

There are several warnings in the Gospels about the spiritual challenges posed by wealth. Our Lord spoke of the "deceitfulness of riches" (Matthew 13:22), and the rich ruler who asked Jesus, apparently sincerely, what he must do to inherit eternal life was told that he must divest himself of his wealth and give it to the poor (Luke 18:18-23). That exchange brought forth from Jesus a graphic word picture in which our Lord challenged the conventional view that wealth was a sign of divine favour: "It is easier for a camel to go through the eye of a needle than for a rich man to enter the kingdom of God" (verse 25).

Luke's presentation of the beatitudes differs from Matthew's in that the positive statements of our Lord which highlight the blessings of those who respond in faith to the Gospel are followed by a matching set of negative statements which draw attention to the curses that shall come upon those who reject it. Luke also appears, through both the order in which he records them and the wording used, to have taken pains to ensure they reflect or echo the message of Mary in her song:

"Blessed are you poor, for yours is the kingdom of God. Blessed are you who hunger now, for you shall be filled." (Luke 6:20,21)

"But woe to you who are rich, for you have received your consolation. Woe to you who are full, for you shall hunger." (Luke 6:24,25)

It seems likely that our Lord was conscious of his family circumstances when he uttered the beatitudes, and we shall return to this theme.

His servant Israel

In the climax of her song in verses 54 and 55 Mary returned to allusions to the covenants:

"He has helped his servant Israel, in remembrance of his mercy, as he spoke to our fathers, to Abraham and to his seed forever." (Luke 1:54,55)

"Helped" doesn't quite capture the richness of this rare word (used only three times in the Bible). In Greek it is *antilambanomai*, which means 'to take hold of in turn, i.e., to succour'. The idea of taking hold is suggestive of hands. It seems likely that this obscure word was used by Mary to build on the concept of the mighty arm of God being revealed both to scatter the proud and to help His servant Israel.

The reference to God's "servant Israel" takes the mind back to the servant prophecies of Isaiah and their rich messianic themes, which must have been familiar to Mary. In Isaiah 41 there are several verses with links to the imagery of the Song of Mary:

"But you, Israel, are my servant, Jacob whom I have chosen, the descendants of Abraham my friend." (verse 8)

"Fear not, for I am with you; be not dismayed, for I am your God. I will strengthen you, yes, I will help you, I will uphold you with my righteous right hand." (verse 10)

"For I, the LORD your God, will hold your right hand, saying to you, 'Fear not, I will help you. Fear not, you worm Jacob, you men of Israel! I will help you,' says the LORD and your Redeemer, the Holy One of Israel." (verses 13,14)

God promised to take His servant Israel by the hand, in particular His right hand which is Christ, and redeem them. And in chapter 42 the prophet identified the Lord Jesus Christ as the pre-eminent servant of God who is taken by the hand:

"I, the LORD, have called you in righteousness, and will hold your hand; I will keep you and give you as a covenant to the people, as a light to the Gentiles."

(verse 6)

Mary spoke both of faithful Israelites in general, and of her son in particular, as being helped by God. The Almighty acts in this way "in remembrance of his mercy". We have already seen that Mary probably drew this thought from Psalm 98:3 ("He has remembered his mercy and his faithfulness to the house of Israel"). It is possible that Mary may also have been alluding to a verse in Micah that touches on this theme. At the very end of Micah there is a passage of which Mary might also have been conscious as she spoke to Elizabeth. The ideas in these verses provide the glue that unites verses 54 and 55 in Mary's song:

"Who is a God like you, pardoning iniquity and passing over the transgression of the remnant of his heritage? He does not retain his anger forever, because he delights in mercy. He will again have compassion on us, and will subdue our iniquities. You will cast all our sins into the depths of the sea. You will give truth to Jacob and mercy to Abraham, which you have sworn to our fathers from days of old."

(Micah 7:18-20)

Micah takes up the theme of truth and mercy that is central to Psalm 98 and links it overtly to forgiveness and to the Abrahamic covenant, just as Mary did in her song. Mercy is fundamental to the Abrahamic covenant. Perhaps both Micah and Mary had a passage from the Pentateuch in mind when they spoke their words:

"(For the LORD your God is a merciful God), he will not forsake you nor destroy you, nor forget the

covenant of your fathers which he swore to them."
(Deuteronomy 4:31)

Here in the reiteration of the Law of Moses at the end of the wilderness wanderings there is a direct link to the covenant to Abraham. The promises made to Abraham, including the mercy which is inherent in them, were made to his seed. Paul says in Galatians 3:16 that Abraham's seed was Christ. Mary concluded her song with a reference to that seed. We can only begin to imagine what lofty thoughts enveloped Mary as she referred to the seed of Abraham, knowing that that seed was even then developing in her womb. And the individual seed then gestating in her womb would one day grow to encompass a multitude – both Jews and Gentiles as Isaiah 42:6 makes plain – who embrace the faith of Abraham.

6

THE SONG OF MARY AND
THE SONG OF HANNAH

"My heart rejoices in the LORD"   (1 Samuel 2:1)

IT was suggested previously that Mary would have left Nazareth immediately upon hearing from Gabriel news of the blessing extended to Elizabeth. It would have taken her several days to reach the hill country of Judea and the sanctuary of Elizabeth's devout and priestly home. On the way her fertile and spiritual mind must have been abuzz with questions, speculations and meditations. Scripturally alert as we know Mary was, her thoughts must have turned to examples of divine intervention in the lives of the faithful, and in particular to instances where God had intervened to effect a miraculous conception.

The case of Sarah must have come to mind. That miracle is central to the theme of the seed of Abraham, a theme taken up in Mary's song, and Gabriel had made a clear allusion to Sarah's divinely-enabled conception in Luke 1:37 ("For with God nothing will be impossible"). But Sarah was an elderly woman of great estate and highly regarded. She was firmly at the centre of ecclesial life at the time. Mary is unlikely, therefore, to have seen Sarah's as a case which closely paralleled her own situation.

In the days of the Judges an angel had appeared to the wife of Manoah and promised her a son who would be devoted to the service of God (as a Nazarite) and who would "begin to deliver Israel" (Judges 13:3-5). Mary may well have contemplated this case because she too was willing for her son to be devoted to God's service, although not necessarily in the extremely ascetic fashion in which a Nazarite served God. But she might not have felt so comfortable about equating her son with Samson, who although a great deliverer of Israel, was something of a moral enigma.

In Hannah, however, there was a case with which Mary might have felt a special bond, for in the story of Hannah and Samuel is combined a woman despised and a son devoted to the service of God. None of the miraculous conceptions in the Old Testament involved a virgin. Hannah, however, knew something of the taunting to which Mary would be exposed because of the cruel scorn directed to her by Peninnah (1 Samuel 1:6). Mary must also later have had cause to compare herself with Hannah when she considered the remarkable degree of support provided by Joseph, who like Elkanah stood by her when she was the victim of vicious taunts.

It is obvious that both women were deeply spiritual. Hannah of course was married and obviously older than Mary because it was already evident that she was barren. In spite of that difference, however, both women were subjects of divine intervention in the provision of a son – in each case a son who would be a spiritual leader for Israel.

1 Samuel 1 presents Hannah deep in silent prayer to God. So intense was her prayer that Eli mistook her demeanour for drunkenness:

"And Hannah answered and said, 'No, my lord, I am a woman of sorrowful spirit. I have drunk neither wine nor intoxicating drink, but have poured out my soul before the LORD. Do not consider your maidservant a wicked woman, for out of the abundance of my complaint and grief I have spoken until now.' Then Eli answered and said, 'Go in peace, and the God of Israel grant your petition which you have asked of him.' And she said, 'Let your maidservant find favour in your sight.' So the woman went her way and ate, and her face was no longer sad." (1 Samuel 1:15-18)

Twice Hannah identified herself as a maidservant, just as Mary did. Eli witnessed this heartfelt prayer and spoke with Hannah before dismissing her with a blessing (1 Samuel 1:17). And note the dignified composure of Hannah's response in verse 18 to the words, not of an angel, but of Eli: they are so reminiscent of Mary's response to Gabriel. Hannah's response to this benediction foreshadowed the language used of Mary in Luke 1: Mary as God's maidservant was "much graced" (Luke 1:28, AV margin) and this earlier maidservant Hannah likewise found grace in God's sight.

The song of Mary takes the reader on a whirlwind tour of the Old Testament doctrine of redemption; we marvel at the spiritual insights of an impoverished teenage Jewess who grew up in an obscure village in Galilee. In addition to quoting a wide range of scripture as outlined in the previous chapter we mentioned in passing that Mary had patterned her song on that of Hannah in 1 Samuel 2. There are some remarkable parallels.

In 1 Samuel 2:1-10 Hannah in prayer sang of her joy at being given a son:

"My heart rejoices in the LORD; my horn is exalted in the LORD. I smile at my enemies, because I rejoice in your salvation. No one is holy like the LORD, for there is none besides you, nor is there any rock like our God. Talk no more so very proudly; let no arrogance come from your mouth, for the LORD is the God of knowledge; and by him actions are weighed. The bows of the mighty men are broken, and those who stumbled are girded with strength. Those who were full have hired themselves out for bread, and the hungry have ceased to hunger. Even the barren has borne seven, and she who has many children has become feeble. The LORD kills and makes alive; he brings down to the grave and brings up. The LORD makes poor and makes rich; he brings low and lifts up. He raises the poor from the dust, and lifts the beggar from the ash heap, to set them among princes and make them inherit the throne of glory. For the pillars of the earth are the LORD's, and he has set the world upon them. He will guard the feet of his saints, but the wicked shall be silent in darkness. For by strength no man shall prevail. The adversaries of the LORD shall be broken in pieces; from heaven he will thunder against them. The LORD will judge the ends of the earth. He will give strength to his king, and exalt the horn of his anointed."

There are clear links between the songs of Mary and of Hannah. Not every verse has a direct link to Hannah's song, nor are the ideas in the same order; both songs, however, cover broadly similar ground. Surely Mary was deeply conscious of Hannah as she expressed herself in the words recorded in Luke 1.

	Luke 1		**1 Samuel 2**
46 47	"And Mary said, *'My soul magnifies* the Lord, and my spirit has rejoiced in God my *Saviour.'"*	1	"And Hannah prayed, and said: *'My heart rejoices* in the LORD; my horn is exalted in the LORD. I smile at my enemies, because I rejoice in your *salvation.'"*
48	"For he has regarded the lowly state of his maidservant; for behold, henceforth all generations will call me blessed."		
49	"For he who is mighty has done great things for me, and *holy is his name."*	2	*"No one is holy* like the LORD, for there is none besides you, nor is there any rock like our God."
50	"And his mercy is on those who fear him from generation to generation."		

51	"He has *shown strength with his arm*;	4	"The bows of the mighty men are broken, and *those who stumbled are girded with strength*."
	he has *scattered the proud* in the imagination of their hearts."	3	*"Talk no more so very proudly*; let no arrogance come from your mouth, for the LORD is the God of knowledge; and by him actions are weighed."
52	"He has *put down the mighty from their thrones*,	4	*"The bows of the mighty men are broken*, and those who stumbled are girded with strength."
	and *exalted the lowly*."	8	*"He raises the poor from the dust and lifts the beggar from the ash heap*, to set them among princes and make them inherit the throne of glory. 'For the pillars of the earth are the LORD's.'"
53	"He has *filled the hungry with good things*, and the rich he has sent away empty."	5	*"Those who were full have hired themselves out for bread*, and *the hungry have ceased to hunger*. Even the barren has borne seven, and she who has many children has become feeble."
54	"He has helped his servant Israel, in remembrance of his mercy;"		
55	"As he spoke to our fathers, to Abraham and to his seed for ever."		

Hannah gave up her son to the service of God:

> "And she said, 'O my lord! As your soul lives, my lord, I am the woman who stood by you here, praying to the LORD. For this child I prayed; and the LORD has granted me my petition which I asked of him. Therefore I also have lent him to the LORD; as long as he lives he shall be lent to the LORD.' So they worshipped the LORD there."   (1 Samuel 1:26-28)

In this respect Hannah and Mary are alike. Mary was required to lend her son to God for "as long as he lives" – in Mary's case quite literally. Hannah's sacrifice must have involved considerable heartache for a woman who was otherwise barren. Even though Mary was not barren like Hannah her sacrifice also came at considerable cost.

In favour with God and man

"And the child Samuel grew on, and was in favour both with the LORD, and also with men" (1 Samuel 2:26). An echo of this may be heard in Proverbs 3:3,4:

> "Let not mercy and truth forsake you; bind them around your neck, write them upon the tablet of your heart, and so find favour and high esteem in the sight of God and man."

Clearly Samuel grew not just naturally but in his appreciation of the ways of God. Mercy and truth were central to his life: they were obvious in his daily life (bound about his neck) and they found a home in his heart. Thus he received the favour of both men and God. The phrase "mercy and truth" is often used of the character of God.[33] In combination in the life of the servants of God mercy and truth are able to purge iniquity (Proverbs 16:6).

An even louder echo of both this testimony about Samuel and of the words in Proverbs is heard in Luke 2, where we read that the twelve-year-old Jesus, like Samuel, developed "in favour with God and men" (Luke

---

33 – See, for example, Genesis 24:27; 32:10; Exodus 34:6; Psalm 25:10.

2:52, RV).[34] This is a remarkable testimony. We can readily understand that Jesus would be favoured by his heavenly Father but Luke says he was also in favour with men – presumably the ordinary men and women with whom he mixed in Nazareth and Galilee.

Notwithstanding the innuendo which we know continued to circulate about his origin, the Nazarenes would recognise and respect a diligent and honest tradesman. They would also honour the care we may presume he showed towards his widowed mother as he became the family bread-winner following Joseph's death; in accordance with his Father's principles, the care of 'the fatherless and the widowed' would have been a high priority for Jesus – which was not always the case with other religiously-inclined men (see Mark 7:11-13). Although his townsfolk would later express reservations about Jesus during his messianic ministry, it is recorded that this was because they had been very familiar with him as a humble carpenter in the midst. Whilst still among them in that role they held Jesus in justifiably high regard, an indirect commendation of Mary as well as of Jesus.

---

34 – Note the plural "men" rather than singular "man" of the AV.

7

A SIGN WHICH SHALL BE SPOKEN AGAINST

"... though you were angry with me, your anger is turned away, and you comfort me." (Isaiah 12:1)

AFTER Mary concluded her song, Luke says (Luke 1:56) that she stayed with Elizabeth for three months and then returned to her house in Nazareth. It must have been some time after her return that Joseph discovered Mary was pregnant, was reassured by the angel and subsequently married her as recorded in Matthew 1. She then came formally into Joseph's house and under his protection.

To Bethlehem

Luke 2 opens with the decree by Caesar Augustus for a census of the empire. It is generally thought that Jesus was born in about September, which would be an ideal time for a census. How do we picture this census? Do we imagine that all over the world people migrated to their ancestral homes? That is highly unlikely. Almost certainly there would be no need for women and children to accompany those men who did have to travel. But in verse 5 Joseph took Mary, in the advanced stages of pregnancy, on a discretionary journey of several days through rugged country. Why?

We are not told why Joseph took Mary with him. Perhaps he wished to combine the journey with celebration at the Temple on the Day of Atonement and of the subsequent feast of tabernacles. Perhaps, in view of the unique circumstances of this impending birth, Joseph and Mary were determined to fulfil Mary's post-natal purification to the best of their ability by attendance at the Temple. Certainly they lingered in the region of Bethlehem and Jerusalem for a prolonged

61

time. Perhaps Joseph wanted to shield Mary from the continuing curiosity of their neighbours in Nazareth. Or was it because they understood the prophecy in Micah 5:2 that Messiah must be born in Bethlehem? Given her deep spiritual understanding as revealed in the song of Mary where there was at least one direct quote from Micah that may be quite possible.

Joseph and Mary reached Bethlehem but could not find suitable accommodation. Mary was obliged to give birth in a place where domestic animals were housed. There is always a degree of anxiety associated with childbirth, especially for the birth of a woman's first child. This must have been heightened in Mary's case by the unfamiliar surroundings and the wondrous nature of the babe to be delivered.

From the language in Luke 2:7 it seems that Mary was unattended when giving birth: "she (i.e. Mary, not a midwife) brought forth her firstborn son, and wrapped him in swaddling cloths, and laid him in a manger". We cannot be dogmatic, but surely it is likely that if Mary had been attended by a midwife that person would have wrapped the new-born baby for her. And the manger, or stall, in which the babe was laid was intended for a domestic animal. Now it is hastily adapted to become the lodging place of one who would be the King of kings and Saviour of the world. This most momentous of all births took place in extraordinarily humble circumstances!

What must Mary have thought as she looked at her newborn son? The usual powerful emotions associated with childbirth must have been accentuated for her. One writer has contemplated her feelings at this time:

"Mothers make a maternal inventory of their baby's toes and fingers and other delightful parts and details; her newborn baby's physical perfection must have brought special wonder to Mary, because she knew that he had no father in the usual sense."[35]

---

35 – Peggy Price, 'Mary, the Mother of Jesus', *Women of the Bible*, page 171.

In verses 10-12 a group of shepherds was told that the Messiah had been born and was lying in a manger. The magi in Matthew 2 told Herod they were on their way to see the baby that was "born king of the Jews" (Matthew 2:2). The angels addressing the shepherds identified the babe as "Christ the Lord". Yet Jesus, born a king, born a lord, was placed in an animal's stall for want of better accommodation. He was not to be found in Herod's palace. He was not securely and comfortably ensconced in the house of the high priest in Jerusalem. Surely God uses the base and weak things of this world to confound the mighty.

The shepherds
We see further evidence of God's elevation of the lowly in the people who were the first to be told of the birth. We tend to have romantic and positive views about shepherds – perhaps derived from scriptural references to God and Christ as shepherds, and the image of David, the shepherd king. In the Holy Land in the first century, however, shepherds tended to be despised. The nature of their work meant it was impossible for them to keep all the ceremonial laws. They had a reputation for being unreliable and untrustworthy because as they moved about the landscape many of them took liberties with the property of others. They were not allowed to give testimony in a court of law, so low was the esteem in which they were held.

Yet it was to such men, keeping watch over flocks, that the angels revealed their astonishing tidings. Possibly, given its close proximity to Jerusalem, the flocks they supervised were sheep intended for sacrifice at the Temple. Now they are called away to meet and worship the Lamb of God, the lamb slain from the foundation of the world, the lamb which would render obsolete the flocks with which they were entrusted.

In verse 11 the angel said to the shepherds, "there is born to you this day ...": to all Israel of course, but perhaps in a special sense to the shepherds. They were given no specific directions for finding the baby, yet in verses 15,16 they went straight to the child and his mother. Did the primitive shelter the family had been forced to use belong to the shepherds? Was it their 'home base'? We cannot be certain but how appropriate if it were! The one who would be King of kings and Lord of lords born in humble circumstances in the premises of despised shepherds, rather than in the splendour of Jerusalem! And where was he to grow up? In despised Nazareth, in lowly esteemed Galilee.

Israel was waiting for Messiah. The nation groaned under the oppression of the Romans and of a corrupt and effete priesthood. The more astute among them knew from the prophets that the time was right for Messiah to appear. The words of the angel in verse 10 were most apt therefore: the news that Messiah had been born really was "good tidings of great joy ...". But the angel's message did not stop there. He completed the statement by adding, "...which will be to all people". The initial angelic message was amplified in verse 14 by the heavenly host (verse 15 makes it clear that this was a host of angels):

"Glory to God in the highest, and on earth peace among men in whom he is well pleased." (RV)

The Revised Version here probably is more accurate. Peace – reconciliation or atonement – is available through the Lord Jesus Christ to those who heed God's call and acknowledge Him as their Sovereign and their Saviour. Whatever the doctrinal significance of these words, however, the message was one of joy for the shepherds and remains a message of joy for us. Israel was waiting for its Messiah, but when he came he brought peace for all men – Jews and Gentiles. Faithful saints in every generation testify to that fact, and seek to be among those referred to in verse 14.

Having heard the message of the "heavenly host" the shepherds went without delay to Mary and the baby Jesus. They felt compelled to share with all who would listen to them the amazing news they had received (verse 17). We can understand the comment in verse 18 that all who heard their testimony "marvelled at those things". By any standard this was astonishing news. But one listener found their message particularly interesting: "Mary kept all these things and pondered them in her heart" (verse 19).

Pondered these things

"These things" (Greek, *rhema*) means 'words'; in this case the words the shepherds relayed from the angels. Luke is making the point that it was not the experience of the shepherds that intrigued Mary so much as the specific words they reported.

Mary kept the words of the shepherds and "pondered them in her heart" (J B Phillips, "turned them over in her mind"; Weymouth, "often dwelling on them in her mind"). In the Greek the word is *sumballo*, which Thayer says means 'to throw together, to bring together'. Rotherham says she was "putting them together in her heart". We may be confident that this was a process that lasted a lifetime. The astonishing news Mary had received in the past nine months had been expressed in straightforward terms, but the use of direct and simple language did not make it easy to comprehend. It is not surprising that the full implications of all that she heard directly from the angel Gabriel and via other divinely directed messengers took some time to unfold. There is, however, a discernible maturing in her mental processes: Mary started out agitated and troubled but now she is compiling a catalogue of these remarkable statements in an effort to comprehend.

Thoughtful Mary			
Passage	NKJV	Greek	Thayer
Luke 1:29	"considered"	*diataratto*	To agitate greatly
Luke 2:19	"pondered them in her heart"	*sumballo*	To throw together, to bring together

In verse 21 Mary and Joseph obeyed God's command when they circumcised and named the baby Jesus as the angel had instructed them. In verse 22, when Jesus was forty days old, Mary and Joseph went to Jerusalem to present the baby formally to his heavenly Father and to offer a sacrifice for cleansing from childbirth and five shekels for the redemption of Mary's firstborn son. Jesus was made of a woman, made under the law, as Paul told the Galatians (4:4). Verse 23 specifically reminds us that the Law of Moses said every firstborn male child was holy to the Lord: none more so than this one.

Mary and Joseph offered as their sacrifice a pair of turtledoves. This was the offering of the very poorest Israelites (Leviticus 12:6-8). Had they had the funds the offering should have been a lamb and a turtledove. Obviously the magi had not yet visited Mary and Jesus for had they done so Mary and Joseph would have been able to offer the more expensive sacrifice. We have already considered the wisdom of God in choosing a poor family to be the guardians of his son. In any event, what need was there for a lamb – they were carrying the true lamb in their arms!

Waiting for the consolation of Israel

In verse 25 Mary and Joseph encounter Simeon at the Temple. Simeon sometimes is thought of as an elderly man but there is no support for that idea. No hint is provided as to his age. Simeon is, however, described as devout and as a man waiting for the "consolation of Israel", which as we shall see means the Messiah. He is described in the inspired record as "just", a word used only of a select handful of individuals[36] and of the immortalised saints.

The Holy Spirit was upon Simeon that day when he encountered Mary and Joseph with the baby Jesus. Perhaps this was a special outpouring of the Holy Spirit

36 – It is used of Joseph (Matthew 1:19), Abel (23:35), Jesus (27:19,24; Luke 23:47), John the Baptist (Mark 6:20), God (John 17:25), Cornelius (Acts 10:22) and Lot (2 Peter 2:7,8).

for there were at this time no Israelites who had the Holy Spirit as a permanent gift as, for instance, was the case after Pentecost. Alternatively, Simeon's heart and mind may have been prepared through his study of the scripture to anticipate the birth of the Messiah just as the magi, as we shall see, anticipated Messiah's birth and recognised that the time was right. This might also help to explain the statement in Luke 2:26 that the Holy Spirit had revealed to Simeon that he would not see death until he had seen the Christ and also his words in verse 30 that he had seen God's salvation.

In Jacob's prophecy in Genesis 49 there is a remarkable verse which appears to stand alone and unconnected to the other verses which relate to the various sons of Jacob and which may in fact relate to Simeon: "I have waited for your salvation, O LORD" (verse 18). Did Simeon see himself as aligned with Jacob who, in his declining years, was given a vision of the great king that God would raise up to deliver his people? Perhaps he did. Now his years of waiting were at an end: the vision given to Jacob was now before his eyes a living and breathing reality.

Waiting is the lot of the faithful in every generation. Simeon was waiting for "the consolation (Greek, *paraklesis*) of Israel". It seems certain that this concept is drawn from Isaiah's servant prophecy; the phrase "consolation of Israel" in particular is redolent of the opening words of Isaiah's servant prophecy, that section of Isaiah which reveals so much about the suffering servant and his role in delivering Israel:

> "'Comfort, yes, comfort my people!' says your God. 'Speak comfort to Jerusalem, and cry out to her, that her warfare is ended, that her iniquity is pardoned; for she has received of the LORD's hand double for all her sins.'" (Isaiah 40:1,2)

The word "comfort" in the Septuagint version of Isaiah 40 is *parakaleite*, a variant form of the *parakelesis* used by Simeon. And how were the people to be comforted?

By the forgiveness of their sins, as the prophet had earlier stated:

> "In that day you will say: 'O LORD, I will praise you; though you were angry with me, your anger is turned away, and you comfort me. Behold, God is my salvation ...'" (Isaiah 12:1,2)

The forgiveness extended through the Messiah had a particular relevance for the city of Jerusalem in which this incident now transpires, but it also has application beyond that city, extending even to those who were afar off, as Simeon would go on to point out in his declaration. Isaiah also took up that theme:

> "Break forth into joy, sing together, you waste places of Jerusalem! For the LORD has comforted his people, he has redeemed Jerusalem. The LORD has made bare his holy arm in the eyes of all the nations; and all the ends of the earth shall see the salvation of our God." (Isaiah 52:9,10)

The whole of the record of Simeon's encounter with Jesus is heavy with allusions to the book of Isaiah, as the following chart, which is adapted from one by George Booker,[37] demonstrates:

	Luke 2		**Isaiah**
26	"And it had been revealed to him by the Holy Spirit that he would not see death before he had seen the Lord's Christ."	61:1	"The spirit of the Lord GOD is upon me, because the LORD has anointed me to preach good tidings."

---

37 – G. Booker, *Unto Us a Child is Born* ..., page 37.

	Luke 2		Isaiah
27	"So he came by the Spirit into the temple. And when the parents brought in the child Jesus, to do for him according to the custom of the law,"	6:1,3,5	"The Lord … [in] the temple … Holy, holy, holy … for my eyes have seen the king."
28	"he took him up in his arms and blessed God and said:"		
29	"Lord, now you are letting your servant depart in peace, according to your word;"	57:1,2	"The righteous perishes … merciful men are taken away … from evil. He shall enter into peace."
30	"For my eyes have seen your salvation,"	62:11	"Surely your salvation is coming."
		52:10	"All the ends of the earth shall see the salvation of our God."
31	"Which you have prepared before the face of all peoples,"	52:10	"The LORD has made bare his holy arm in the eyes of all the nations;"

	Luke 2		Isaiah
32	"A light to bring revelation to the Gentiles ..."	42:6	"... as a light to the Gentiles."
		49:6	"I will also give you as a light to the Gentiles."
		60:1,3	"Your light has come ... The Gentiles shall come to your light."
	"... and the glory of your people Israel."	45:25	"In the LORD all the descendants of Israel shall be justified, and shall glory."
33	"And Joseph and his mother marvelled at those things which were spoken of him."		
34	"Then Simeon blessed them, and said to Mary his mother, 'Behold, this child is destined for the fall ..."	8:14, 15	"A stone of stumbling and a rock of offence to both the houses of Israel ... many among them shall stumble; they shall fall."
	"... and rising of many in Israel ..."	26:19	"Your dead shall live; together with my dead body they shall arise."
	"... and for a sign which will be spoken against.'"	7:14	"A sign; Behold, the virgin shall conceive and bear a son."

	Luke 2		Isaiah
35	"(Yes, a sword will pierce through your own soul also), that the thoughts of many hearts may be revealed."	8:18	"I and the children whom the LORD has given me! We are for signs and for wonders."
		53:5, 7,8	"Wounded for our transgressions, ... oppressed ... afflicted ... cut off from the land of the living."

Simeon had a lively faith in the promised Messiah and he had been waiting. He now knew the truth of Isaiah's words that "they shall not be ashamed who wait for me" (Isaiah 49:23). The same is true of those who, like Simeon, are today still waiting for the "consolation of Israel".

The Holy Spirit had told Simeon that he would see the Messiah before he died. When he saw Jesus he took the child and proclaimed in Luke 2:29-32:

"Lord, now you are letting your servant depart in peace, according to your word; for my eyes have seen your salvation, which you have prepared before the face of all peoples, a light to bring revelation to the Gentiles, and the glory of your people Israel."

Verse 29 explains what the "consolation of Israel" meant to Simeon. Farrer[38] says verse 29 should be rendered: "Now art thou setting free thy slave, O Master, according to thy word, in peace". The word 'depart' is the Greek word *apoluo* which Thayer says means 'to set free'. Bullinger defines it as 'to loose from, set free, release from'. The same word is used of the release of Barabbas (Mark 15:11,15; Luke 23:17,18,25).

---

38 – F. W. Farrar, St. Luke, (*Cambridge Bible for Schools and Colleges*), page 72.

'May I see the consolation of Israel', was a Jewish prayer pleading for the advent of Messiah, and the Hebrew name 'Menachem', which means consolation, was used by the rabbis as a title of the Messiah.

Simeon recognised that this baby was indeed Messiah and that it was he who would deliver ("set free") the faithful from bondage to sin and death. And although the one in his arms was but an infant, Simeon knew that nothing would impede God's redemptive work. Thus verse 30 refers to salvation as a present reality. In verses 31 and 32 Simeon acknowledged that the ministry of Jesus is for all men, Jews and Gentiles. The Lord's disciples struggled with the idea of the Gospel going forth to the Gentiles but we have seen through a consideration of the song of Mary and it is clear in the servant prophecies that this concept is firmly rooted in the Old Testament, and indeed in the Abrahamic covenant.

In verse 33 Joseph and Mary marvelled at Simeon's message. As with the message from the shepherds, we should not assume that anything Simeon said was unknown to Mary and Joseph, but the accumulation of all these astonishing statements about their baby must have been overwhelming. More material for Mary to ponder!

A sign which will be spoken against

In verse 34 Simeon made a comment about the life and mission of Jesus and in verse 35 he made a specific comment about Mary:

> "Then Simeon blessed them, and said to Mary his mother, 'Behold, this child is destined for the fall and rising of many in Israel, and for a sign which will be spoken against (yes, a sword will pierce through your own soul also), that the thoughts of many hearts may be revealed."

We know the truth of verse 34. Many of Israel's leaders stumbled at the Lord as 'a rock of offence'. In later times many Gentiles would like likewise stumble.

Many others in Israel, however, responded to his preaching and have risen to heavenly places in Christ Jesus, and will rise even more completely and permanently in the resurrection.

The phrase, "a sign which will be spoken against", is significant. The miraculous nature of the conception of Jesus was a sign to the nation, as Isaiah had predicted – "the virgin shall conceive and bear a Son" (7:14). The concept of a child as a sign is also found elsewhere in the prophecy of Isaiah, where the prophet's sons were signs for Israel (8:18). Just as the names of Isaiah's sons – Shear-jashub and Maher-shalal-hash-baz[39] – embodied a message for Judah about impending divine judgment, so the name of Mary's son bore a similar message for Judea – Yahweh (Israel's God) shall save.

Now the sign had been fulfilled, and what happened? Mary suffered horribly at the hands of malicious gossips while carrying her child. It is clear from John 8 that this vicious innuendo about Mary's morality persisted for many years. In a society where illegitimacy carried such a terrible stigma, claims about improper conduct took a heavy toll on the victims. In John 8 one of the tactics used by the Jewish leaders to undermine support for Jesus was the questioning of his legitimacy:

"Then they said to him, 'We were not born of fornication; we have one Father – God.'" (John 8:41)

We may be certain that this accusation was not just spoken to Jesus. It would have been surreptitiously spread abroad to any who would listen. For Mary it must have seemed like she would never be free of this whispering campaign. Truly hers was a sign that was spoken against – both in the lead-up to the birth of Jesus and for more than 30 years afterwards.

There is another sense in which the sign was spoken against. The phrase "spoken against" was used later in Acts 28:22 where Luke says the Jews in Rome wanted

---

39 – 'The remnant shall return' and 'Speed the spoil, hasten the prey'.

to know about the sect that is "is spoken against everywhere". In his lifetime the Jewish leaders spoke of Jesus as "that deceiver" (Matthew 27:63), "a Samaritan" (John 8:48) and one who "has a demon" (John 10:20). Years after his death they were still unable to speak civilly about our Lord. In the Talmud Jesus is never mentioned directly by name; he is alluded to by expressions such as 'so and so', 'that man', 'Absalom' and 'the hung'.[40] And in the secular world today Jesus is still spoken against, as are the modern signs that relate not to his first advent but to his near return.

Simeon in verse 35 concluded with poignant words for Mary. "Yes, a sword will pierce through your own soul also". It was clear from verse 34 that our Lord was to find himself in conflict with the authorities. Mary is now told that he would not suffer alone. She also would feel much of the pain and many of the blows that would be inflicted on her son. Some of these blows would come through her own imperfect comprehension of his role and mission, while others as we have seen would come upon her without any just cause.

In spite of the great challenges Mary would face, God's overshadowing care for his handmaid is evident in so many apparently insignificant ways. The ominous words with which Simeon concluded might have left Mary feeling morose and troubled but for an encounter she had "that instant" (i.e., immediately after Simeon finished speaking) with Anna. This aged faithful widow had similar faith and insight to that which Simeon had displayed:

"Now there was one, Anna, a prophetess, the daughter of Phanuel, of the tribe of Asher. She was of a great age, and had lived with a husband seven years from her virginity; and this woman was a widow of about eighty-four years, who did not depart from the temple, but served God with fastings and

40 – See F. W. Farrar, St Luke, (*Cambridge Bible for Schools and Colleges*), page 73.

prayers night and day. And coming in that instant she gave thanks to the Lord, and spoke of him to all those who looked for redemption in Jerusalem."

(verses 36-38)

Anna must have been attracted to what Simeon was doing with and saying about this infant. It is not certain what we are to make of Anna's designation as a prophetess unless we are to understand it as applying to her in this incident specifically, for there is no other record of a divinely inspired spokesperson (of either gender) at this time. Whatever the term might have meant up to that point, however, upon encountering the baby Jesus Anna uttered a divinely-inspired message about redemption available through Mary's son. Such a testimony from a woman who must have been extremely well-known and respected by the Temple worshippers would have a profound impact on all who witnessed the scene.

Luke specifically links Anna and Simeon during this first visit of the family to the Temple. No doubt there were others, in particular the priests on duty, with whom the family would have interacted during their visit, but these two are mentioned in particular. That would seem to be an echo of another of Isaiah's messianic prophecies (note the use of plural terms in verse 8):

"Your watchmen shall lift up their voices, with their voices shall they sing together; for they shall see eye to eye when the LORD brings back Zion. Break forth into joy, sing together, you waste places of Jerusalem! For the LORD has comforted his people, he has redeemed Jerusalem." (Isaiah 52:8,9)

Given this, it is not surprising that Luke tells us Anna spoke about the child Jesus to "all that looked for redemption in Jerusalem", a term which hearkens back to the comfort Messiah would bring to Israel when "the LORD has comforted his people" and "has redeemed Jerusalem" (Isaiah 52:9).

It would have been with mixed emotions that Mary and Joseph left the Temple and returned to Bethlehem. So much had happened in the past year. They had both heard many remarkable things, especially during the visit to the Temple. The record refers on more than one occasion to how Mary cogitated on the things she was told. William Ramsay draws attention to the mental turmoil this entailed for Mary:

"Mary apparently did not even tell her husband what was in her mind. This child was not to be an unalloyed delight either to her country or herself; he was 'set for the falling and rising of many in Israel, and for a sign which is spoken against'; and for herself, 'a sword shall pierce through her own soul'. It was a dread and vague future about which she pondered in the depths of her own mind, as the 'child grew and waxed strong, filled with wisdom'. In that marvellous picture, sketched in such simple and brief terms, only he that deliberately shuts his mind against all literary feeling can fail to catch the tone of a mother's heart."[41]

There must have been many nights when Mary lay awake trying to make sense of what had happened to her and what might transpire in the years ahead. There may be no doubt that she would make mention of these matters in her prayers to God. We know that God communicated regularly with His Son to assist him in his earthly ministry. It is impossible, therefore, to believe that God would have left the mother of His Son in total bewilderment and comfortless as she struggled with the challenges she faced as the handmaid of the Lord.

---

41 – William Ramsay, *Was Christ Born at Bethlehem? A Study on the Credibility of St. Luke*, pages 76-77.

8

FROM BETHLEHEM TO NAZARETH

"... when they had performed all things according to the law of the Lord, they returned into Galilee, to their own city, Nazareth."   (Luke 2:39)

WITH the remarkable testimonies of both Simeon and Anna ringing in their ears Mary and Joseph returned to Bethlehem, not Nazareth as Luke might imply. Luke's record compresses the following two years or so into one verse and we need to consider the Matthew record for the intervening events.

It would appear that Mary and Joseph decided to remain in the city of David following the birth of Jesus. Perhaps it was to escape the hurtful gossip in Nazareth, but more likely it was to allow Jesus to grow up where they assumed he should grow up as David's greater son – as the heir to the throne of David. In this way he would be ready to be revealed from Bethlehem Ephratah, in accordance with Micah 5:2.

All mothers cherish their babies, their firstborn always have a special place in their heart and for many women there often is a special bond with a son. How much more in this case for this mother and this baby boy! In her unique circumstances Mary must have spent many hours in wondrous reverie as she nursed the baby Jesus. And the Psalmist records that her maternal care was greatly valued by her son:

"You are he who took me out of the womb; you made me trust while on my mother's breasts. I was cast upon you from birth. From my mother's womb you have been my God."   (Psalm 22:9,10)

From his earliest days our Lord was conscious of the care lavished upon him by his mother.

The magi

Matthew 2 records the visit of "wise men (magi) from the east" (literally, rising). The name magi is derived from a Median tribe and referred to a certain caste of religious men associated with the Zoroastrian religion, astronomy and astrology. The east is an imprecise description of their origin. The word is used in the Septuagint to refer to the wise men of Babylon (Daniel 1:20; 2:2,10,27; 4:4; 5:7,11,15) and is reflected in Babylonian names such as Rab-mag, so it is reasonable to guess that they may have originated in Babylon.

We may speculate that these wise men received some form of divine revelation about a star, but that they may also have been custodians of prophetic knowledge that would have been the legacy of Israel's captivity in Babylon. Daniel had been in charge of the wise men in Babylon (Daniel 2:48) and perhaps their successors still cherished Daniel's words such as those in the seventy weeks prophecy.

It was not just faithful Jews at this time who had great expectations that some form of divine saviour was about to be manifested. William Ramsay commented on this:

> "The belief was widespread in the world at that time or earlier that the Epiphany, or coming of a god in human form on earth, was imminent, in order to save the human race from the destruction which the sins of mankind deserved and had brought nigh. The world was perishing in its crimes, and only the coming of God Himself could save it. This belief can be observed in various forms during the years that proceeded. It prompted the Fourth Eclogue of Virgil and it is seen in the Second Ode of Horace."[42]

42 – William Ramsay, *The Bearing of Recent Discovery on the Trustworthiness of the New Testament*, page 145

It would seem that a combination of expectation, signs and knowledge motivated the magi to depart "from the east" and travel to Jerusalem (Matthew 2:1). They were seeking the king of the Jews so it was only natural that they should go to the capital city of the Jews. That they were Gentiles rather than Jews may be inferred from the fact that, notwithstanding any knowledge they may have had of Daniel's prophecies, they clearly were unaware of Micah's very direct prophecy about the birthplace of the king of the Jews.

There has been much speculation about the "star in the east" the magi told Herod they had seen. Some elaborate attempts have been made to explain it as an astronomical phenomenon but the text in verse 9 speaks of the star guiding them from Jerusalem to the very spot where Jesus could be found. This could not be true of a natural star or other celestial body because the distances involved would preclude such a precise pinpointing on earth.

Whatever the star was, it was a divinely provided and directed source of light, a singularly appropriate tool for directing them to the one who would be the light of the world, "a Star ... out of Jacob; a Sceptre ... out of Israel" (Numbers 24:17).[43] The star and the visit of the magi were a fulfilment of the prophecy of Isaiah 60:1-6:

"Arise, shine; for your light has come! And the glory of the LORD is risen upon you. For behold, the darkness shall cover the earth, and deep darkness the people; but the LORD will arise over you, and his glory will be seen upon you. The Gentiles shall come to your light, and kings to the brightness of your rising ... the wealth of the Gentiles shall come to you ... they shall bring gold and incense, and they shall proclaim the praises of the LORD."

In verse 2 the magi enquired as to the whereabouts of the one who had been "born King of the Jews". Herod,

_____

43 – Balaam's prophecy goes on to state that the "Star out of Jacob" shall conquer Edom (verse 18), an ironic point given Herod's nationality.

always rather paranoid, was greatly troubled when he learnt of their quest and asked the religious leaders for information about the birthplace of Messiah (verse 4); as a Gentile like the magi, Herod also was unaware of Micah's prophecy. He understood only too well, however, what the magi meant when they sought the King of the Jews and the potential implications for him. There is a certain irony, perhaps unintentional, in the contrast between an Idumean who was in effect a usurper on the throne and the one "whose right it is" (Ezekiel 21:27) who was sought by the magi who had been "born King of the Jews". Ironic it might have been, but Herod interpreted it as a threat.

In verse 11, having had their fateful encounter with Herod and been given instructions by him as to where they might find the Messiah, the magi arrived in Bethlehem and came to the place to which the star directed them:

"When they had come into the house, they saw the young child with Mary his mother, and fell down and worshipped him. And when they had opened their treasures, they presented gifts to him: gold, frankincense, and myrrh."

Mary and Joseph appear to have secured a house for themselves and the growing boy, evidence perhaps of their intention to make their home there. At that home the wise men did homage and offered precious gifts – gifts which, even if little more than tokens (as some have suggested), must have been very welcome in such a poor household. It is worth noting in this record that although the magi met with both Mary and Jesus, they "fell down, and worshipped him (i.e., Jesus)", not both Jesus and Mary. Thus there is no incidental support in this encounter for the later cult of Mariolatry that has so besmirched the memory of this wonderful woman.

The chief priests and scribes had no hesitation in answering Herod's question about the birthplace of the Messiah, and the wise men had no hesitation in acting on their information. There is, however, no hint that the religious rulers made steps to visit their young king. Is this a very early indication of their determination to reject the Messiah? Perhaps they were complicit in or at least willing witnesses of Herod's murderous response to the news that the king of Israel had been born in Bethlehem.

Flight into Egypt

After the departure of the magi, Joseph as head of the family received a further divine message in a dream in Matthew 2:13. He was warned to flee from the impending wrath of Herod and take the family to Egypt. The family obeyed without delay, even though travelling with an infant can be exhausting and challenging. There was a well-travelled highway from Judea into Egypt but the journey was long, tiresome and through inhospitable terrain. Being nearly two years since the birth of Jesus it is also possible that Mary had another baby to look after or that she was expecting a child.

It had been daunting enough for Mary to move as a young mother to a strange city like Bethlehem. It seems that they knew no one in that city because they were obliged to resort to an animal enclosure when Mary was giving birth. But at least the people in Bethlehem were fellow Israelites, and many of them of the same lineage. In the months following the birth of Jesus, Mary would have developed a circle of friends, especially among the women who also had babies of much the same age. She would meet them at the well and talk with them while their children played together. Now she is to be uprooted and taken into Egypt where again they would be strangers. And she took with her the foreboding engendered by the dream Joseph received.

Going down into Egypt might have seemed a retrograde step. Israel had come out of Egyptian darkness and Isaiah had condemned those "rebellious children ... who walk to go down to Egypt" (30:1,2) and pronounced: "Woe to those who go down to Egypt for help" (31:1). But Mary and Joseph were acting in response to divine counsel and not their own inclinations as were the people of whom Isaiah spoke. We marvel at the implicit faith demonstrated by both Mary and Joseph in undertaking such a journey.

Scripture is silent when it comes to details of the sojourn in Egypt, both in terms of its duration and the specific locality although tradition says that the family dwelt near Cairo. It is likely that Mary and Joseph would have sought out other faithful Jewish families living in Egypt, for a sizable number of Jews lived in the land. Jews had been migrating to Egypt since before the Babylonian captivity, and there was a significant exodus of Israelites into Egypt after the murder of Gedaliah (2 Kings 25:25,26).

The real influx of Jews into Egypt, however, was triggered by Alexander the Great, who offered Jewish residents of Alexandria the same rights as its Greek citizens. As a consequence of their privileged position in that city and Egypt generally many more Jews fled to Alexandria for refuge from the anti-Semitic aggression of the Seleucid dynasty over the centuries following the death of Alexander the Great.

At the time of Christ it is said that the Jewish population of Egypt was at least one million; one fifth of the population of ancient Alexandria was Jewish and they were among its most influential citizens. Alfred Edersheim says that all shipping within and from Egypt, and the export of grain in particular, was controlled by the Jews, which meant that Jews were responsible for feeding the Roman Empire.[44] It was on grain ships en route from Egypt to Rome that Paul travelled as a prisoner (Acts 27:6 and 28:11).

It is perhaps more than a curious coincidence that the Lord Jesus Christ, whose teachings would later offer the citizens of Rome the bread of life which never perishes, should himself have come out of Egypt. It seems likely that the presence of so many Jews in what

---

44 – Alfred Edersheim, *Sketches of Jewish Social Life in the Days of Christ*, page 208.

was the leading mercantile city of the world at the time of Christ helped to prepare the Greek-speaking world for the preaching of the Apostles.

The Septuagint had been translated in Egypt and Apollos, "an eloquent man and mighty in the scriptures" came from Alexandria (Acts 18:24), so we may be certain that there were many in Egypt with a keen interest in the word of God. Apollos was a faithful Jew who knew the baptism of John (Acts 18:25), so it would seem that at least some of the local Jews had an awareness of and interest in messianic issues.

While in Egypt Mary and Joseph, possibly in fellowship with other faithful Jews, may have pondered Egypt's significance in the Old Testament – Jacob's family finding refuge from famine in Egypt, the condemnation of Egyptian idolatry, Israel's deliverance from Egyptian bondage, the unreliability of Egypt as a partner for Israel. All of these must have featured in their thoughts. And what did they make of Hosea's prophecy, "When Israel was a child, I loved him, and out of Egypt I called my son" (Hosea 11:1)? Surely this must have reassured Mary that the family's residence in Egypt was only temporary.

We see God's providence so clearly in these events. The wise men gave Mary precious gifts which may well have funded their flight and refuge in Egypt; when the threat posed by Herod passed, God could call His Son out of Egypt, as Matthew 2:15 says.

The fact that Herod decided to kill all "male children" (RSV) in Bethlehem under two years old suggests that our Lord might have been nearly two when the family fled into Egypt. Verse 16 is explicit that Herod's age threshold was based on the timing of Christ's birth. Matthew's quotation of Jeremiah 31:15 expresses the intense anguish that this despicably violent act generated in Bethlehem.

Although Mary was spared the indescribable grief of the slaughter of her own baby she must have shared the agonies of the other families in Bethlehem. In the two years of her sojourn in the city of David Mary would have become familiar with the other mothers and their babies. She would have taken an interest in the development of the other children; she would have shared the joys and trials of the other families; her son would have played with the other baby boys. Mary would live for the rest of her life with the knowledge that, although she and Joseph had been warned to flee, all these other families had been afflicted because of her son. Simeon's words must have flooded back into her mind: "a sword shall pierce through your own soul also", as it did so many of the Lord's kinsmen in Bethlehem.

Two more dreams

Joseph received two further divine messages telling the family to return and, later, directing them to Nazareth:

"But when Herod was dead, behold, an angel of the Lord appeared in a dream to Joseph in Egypt, saying, 'Arise, take the young child and his mother, and go to the land of Israel, for those who sought the young child's life are dead.' Then he arose, took the young child and his mother, and came into the land of Israel. But when he heard that Archelaus was reigning over Judea instead of his father Herod, he was afraid to go there. And being warned by God in a dream, he turned aside into the region of Galilee. And he came and dwelt in a city called Nazareth, that it might be fulfilled which was spoken by the prophets, 'He shall be called a Nazarene.'" (Matthew 2:19-23)

Joseph, as head of the family, is the dominant figure in this record: it was to the head of the family that the divine messages came. Mary was submissive towards Joseph as she was towards the angel. She did not allow her blessed state to jaundice her mind towards her husband. A faithful partner, Mary was a model of spiritual integrity.

God called his son out of Egypt. Mary and Joseph seem to have remained convinced that the child should be raised in Bethlehem but were nervous about the influence of the Herod family. The angel confirmed that "they (Herod and his counsellors?) are dead which sought the young child's life", but redirected the family to Nazareth. While Bethlehem figured in the prophets so too did Nazareth, but not in a way which would have been obvious to Mary and Joseph – or indeed to many in Israel without the benefit of the divinely inspired application of the "branch" prophecies in Matthew 2:23. So it was that, apparently against their own will, Mary and Joseph were directed back to where they had started at Nazareth. Presumably Mary and Joseph settled into family life in Nazareth. Joseph supported his growing family as a carpenter and Mary would have found herself fully occupied as a wife and mother of a growing family, and annually they joined with other faithful neighbours for a pilgrimage to Jerusalem to celebrate Passover.

Parental allegiances

There is no reason to believe Mary was flawless. Indeed, it is clear from the record that she had her faults and that she did not always understand what was happening in relation to Jesus. This is seen in the next recorded incident in Mary's life, about nine or ten years later, when Jesus was twelve and Mary and Joseph took their family to Jerusalem for Passover.

As was common practice at the time, Mary and Joseph joined other pilgrims for the annual journey from Galilee to Jerusalem. Some of them may have been relatives from Nazareth while others are likely to have been from other villages. The party would assume a degree of communal responsibility towards all its members. On the return journey from the feast Joseph and Mary became concerned about Jesus when they discovered that he was absent from the travelling party (Luke 2:44,45).

Implicit in these circumstances is an insight into how Mary nurtured the Son of God. Given such a momentous charge some women may have been tempted to cocoon Jesus and treat him as a rare and

precious jewel. It is evident from the arrangements for
this pilgrimage that Mary was not unduly cautious or
over-protective. At twelve years of age she treated Jesus
as any Galilean mother would treat a son of similar age.
Jesus was allowed to mingle with others his age within
the party generally: he was not cosseted by his mother.
All mothers fret about the risks their growing sons take
and we may expect that the unique circumstances
surrounding her firstborn's birth only heightened
Mary's anxieties at times as Jesus grew. It says much
for her character and the wisdom of God's choice that
she allowed Jesus to lead a normal boyhood in the hills
of Galilee and Judea. Had Jesus been brought up in
seclusion from the wider community he would not have
developed the character he required to fulfil his
ministry as an adult.

Jesus had remained behind in Jerusalem to discuss
spiritual matters with the Jewish leaders. Among them
perhaps were some of the men Herod had consulted ten
or eleven years before. Mary and Joseph were forced to
return to Jerusalem to find him.

Mary was separated from her son for three days. Any
parent would be frantic about a child missing for three
days. She must have been nearly hysterical by the time
they located Jesus. He appears to have spent those days
at the Temple on his "Father's business". Perhaps some
21 years later Mary would recall these three anxious
days when she again lost him for exactly that period of
time while he was in the tomb, at the very climax of his
attention to his Father's business.

When they located their boy, Mary rebuked Jesus
and he had to correct their perspective:

"When they saw him, they were amazed; and his
mother said to him, 'Son, why have you done this to
us? Look, your father and I have sought you
anxiously.' And he said to them, 'Why did you seek
me? Did you not know that I must be about my
Father's business?'" (Luke 2:48,49)

Mary and Joseph were "amazed" when they found Jesus engaged in debate with the doctors of the Law. In what way were they amazed? They would not have been amazed at his level of maturity or the depth of his spiritual insight. These were things to which they must have been exposed on a daily basis. Perhaps they were amazed at how dignified and urbane the doctors were in spite of being interrogated and challenged by a mere boy of twelve, not to mention the son of a provincial family from Galilee. The later record suggests that this would not be something with which the lawyers usually were comfortable. Or perhaps they were amazed with themselves for not realising that this was where they should look.

In verse 48 Mary rebuked her son. In relatively gentle terms Jesus corrected his mother (verse 49). She had referred to Joseph as the boy's father and, while it is implicit that Jesus recognised his foster-father's authority in the family, his true Father was God. Although apprenticed to Joseph it was the work of his heavenly Father which must take precedence. In verse 49 Jesus reminded Mary that he had a mission from God and that this must override any earthly ties. Having made that point, however, Jesus returned to Nazareth with Mary and Joseph and was subject to them.

Verse 50 says "they did not understand the words". Here were more words they would add to those on which they pondered. In verse 51 it again says that Mary "kept all these things in her heart". Part of a growing catalogue, these words joined those of the angel, Elizabeth, the shepherds, Simeon and Anna in the library of her mind.

'Cottage home in that despised Nazareth'
Other than the visit to Jerusalem when Jesus was twelve there is no direct reference in scripture to the family life of Mary in Nazareth. We learn from Luke 2:41 that the family made a yearly pilgrimage to Jerusalem to celebrate Passover. They may have

87

attended other religious festivals in Jerusalem also, and as guardians of the Son of God we could imagine that they would see this as appropriate, but the record is silent about such visits.

We may presume that Mary and Joseph lived as best they could in accordance with the Law of Moses. Jesus and his brothers would have attended lessons in the local synagogue. As they matured they would have taken their place in the congregation, with the boys taking their turn to read the scripture at the weekly services.

The books of Kings and Chronicles testify to the powerful influence of mothers on those who became kings in Judah. Mary would be aware of that fact. As she thought about this, some of the words of Solomon in Proverbs may have seemed especially relevant to Mary. Solomon exhorted sons to hearken to the voice of both their parents:

"My son, hear the instruction of your father, and do not forsake the law of your mother."

(Proverbs 1:8 – see also 6:20)

Our Lord certainly was attentive to the instruction of his heavenly Father but we know that he was also subject to his foster father. We must presume that he would also have been responsive to the direction of his mother. The faithful family life of Mary and Joseph would have complemented the divine instruction our Lord received from God. As "Jesus increased in wisdom and stature, and in favour with God and man" he would have brought much joy to his mother and Joseph:

"The father of the righteous will greatly rejoice, and he who begets a wise child will delight in him. Let your father and your mother be glad, and let her who bore you rejoice." (Proverbs 23:24,25)

Joseph's disappearance from the record suggests that some time after the visit to Jerusalem, recorded in Luke 2, Mary was widowed. We know that Mary had at least four other sons and at least two daughters (Matthew 13:55,56) who appear to have reached adulthood, all of them younger than Jesus. It would not be unusual if others had died in infancy. As the oldest son Jesus would have particular responsibilities for his widowed mother and her dependent children.

Jewish lads were taught a trade and Joseph instructed Jesus, and probably his other sons who were old enough, in carpentry. Following his death Jesus and Mary's other sons would have taken over the carpentry shop and continued to assist the townsfolk with the manufacture and repair of agricultural implements and furniture. It is interesting to think that Jesus' first formal experience as a teacher may have been in the workshop in Nazareth imparting carpentry skills to his younger brothers. We may be certain that the Lord's parable about the mote and the beam has a background in these years labouring as a humble carpenter in an obscure village in Galilee.

Carpenters develop a profound appreciation of timber and its properties. They have an admiration for trees and their potential that eludes others unskilled in their craft. Our Lord would thus have had a special affinity for the tree of life. As a carpenter he would have known which timber was best for each purpose. He would have known the strength of nails and the power of woodworking tools. For Jesus, that knowledge must have added to his understanding of what crucifixion would entail. How often as he hammered a nail into a piece of timber did our Lord hear an echo in advance of the thud of nails being driven through his hands and feet into a rough stake? This is further evidence of the providential wisdom of God in choosing both Mary and Joseph to raise His son.

Almost certainly the fact that Jesus' public ministry commenced when he was thirty was intended to mirror the provision in the law that priests commenced their duties at that age. It also meant, however, that he was able to ensure that the welfare of Mary and his younger siblings was properly met. As the son of the One who protects the fatherless and the widowed that was only as it should be. By the time Jesus was thirty at least most of Mary's other children must have reached adulthood and have been able to help look after their ageing mother's needs. He could safely leave the carpenter's shop in the hands of one or more of his half-brothers.

There may be an absence of direct scriptural reference to family life in Nazareth, but the Gospels are suffused with indirect allusions to Mary's home life, which would have mirrored that of other mothers in Nazareth. We are justified perhaps in seeing allusions to it in the teaching of the Master. For instance, his images of two women grinding together (Luke 17:35), the simple oven of a poor family (Matthew 6:30) and the use of leaven in bread-making (Matthew 13:33) may well have been drawn from his observations of his mother.

The Lord's reference to the repair of old clothes (Mark 2:21) may have reminded him of Mary's diligence as a poor housewife trying to make the most of meagre resources but wary also of false economies. Jesus would have remembered Mary sweeping her little dwelling (Luke 11:25), and perhaps he recalled her anxious search for a lost coin (Luke 15:8), which would have been so precious to a poor widow with no other family support.

Jesus was also conscious of the traumas that were the lot of villagers in Galilee. In Luke 7 when Jesus approached the village of Nain he witnessed a funeral procession for the only son of a poor widow (verses 11-15). The record says that Jesus had compassion for the widow and restored him to life. In verse 15 it specifically says that Jesus "presented him to his mother". Although Mary had other sons, the relation-ship of Jesus to Mary as a son was unique. Any mother would be heartbroken by the death of any son, and a woman with only one son especially so. When Jesus saw this funeral procession was he conscious of the pain his mother would experience when he would be crucified? In raising this man to life was he in fact prefiguring the wonderful time when he too would be restored to life?

There are ample allusions in the Lord's ministry that confirm Mary lived a humble village life filled with the limited comforts and abundant frustrations poor women across the Holy Land experienced. Her son referred more readily to things like lamps and bushels (Matthew 5:15) and moth and rust (Matthew 6:19), than to the luxuries that were enjoyed by the elite in Herod's court or among the priestly caste in Jerusalem. With the insight of one who had farmed he referred to the realities of raising crops (Mark 4:28), no doubt recalling his years first assisting Joseph, and then afterwards on his own account, providing for his mother and his brothers and sister. Israel's future king grew up in a climate which equipped him to understand the hopes, aspirations and needs of ordinary men and women and not detached from their affairs as is the case for most monarchs. He still understands the needs of the poor and humble in this age, and we may praise God and thank Mary that this is the case.

In the obscurity of a Galilean backwater Mary lived for many years with her children, poor, thoughtful and faithful, perhaps relishing the tranquillity she knew from the testimony of Simeon could never last.

Mary in the beatitudes

Some of the most famous of the sayings the Lord uttered during his ministry are known as the beatitudes. It was suggested in an earlier chapter that it is likely the sentiments embodied in the beatitudes might have been influenced by the Lord's home life in Nazareth. There are two versions of the beatitudes – that which is found in Matthew 5 at the beginning of the Sermon on the Mount (arguably the better known version) and the one found in Luke 6. Luke is the gospel writer who appears to have the greatest insight into Mary (did he meet Mary in her later years?) and it is interesting to consider how the beatitudes as recorded by Luke might have been informed by the Lord's observation of his mother's life:

91

"Blessed are you poor, for yours is the kingdom of God" (Luke 6:20).	Poverty was no stranger to Mary and her family in Nazareth, but they took comfort in the assurance of the kingdom – a kingdom of which Mary's son was the embodiment.
"Blessed are you who hunger now, for you shall be filled" (verse 21).	Mary referred in her song to the hungry being filled (Luke 1:53) and hunger would also have been a reality at times for her family.
"Blessed are you who weep now, for you shall laugh" (verse 21).	There were many causes for tears as Mary endured the taunts of the ignorant and witnessed the threats to her son.
"Blessed are you when men hate you, and when they exclude you, and revile you, and cast out your name as evil, for the Son of man's sake" (verse 22)	This also was the reality of Mary's life. The target of gossip and innuendo she would have been shunned by the self-righteous. She suffered reproach, and in a very unique and literal way this was for the "Son of man's sake".

Given the applicability of so many of these words to her own circumstances we can well imagine the comfort Mary would draw from the words which followed them: "Rejoice in that day, and leap for joy! for indeed your reward is great in heaven, for in the like manner their fathers did to the prophets" (Luke 6:23). Truly Mary's reward is great and she will yet leap for joy – perhaps more than any other of the resurrected saints – on the resurrection morn.

9

FROM NAZARETH TO GOLGOTHA

"... he steadfastly set his face to go to Jerusalem."
(Luke 9:51)

WHILE we may deduce certain suggestions about life in Nazareth for Mary and Jesus when he was a young man, a veil is drawn in scripture over the actual details of their life. From Jesus at the age of twelve, we do not hear of either of them again until Jesus is baptized at thirty years of age.

At Cana

In John 2 Jesus appears to begin his public ministry immediately after his baptism and temptation in the wilderness. It commenced with his attendance at a wedding in Cana at which Mary accompanied him (John 2:1-5). Cana was a town in Galilee quite close to Nazareth. At this stage there may have been only a few disciples, being those referred to in John 1. Two of these, James and John the sons of Zebedee, were cousins of Jesus. The fact that they and Mary were present suggests that the wedding was that of one of their mutual relations. That might explain Mary's willingness to intervene when the wine ran out – a terrible calamity and a potential embarrassment for a host who may have been a close relative.

As a widow in very humble circumstance and with a large family Mary would have become used to relying on the resourcefulness of Jesus to solve problems at home in Nazareth, especially following the death of Joseph. It was only natural that she should seek his assistance now. It would seem, however, that Mary's comment in verse 3 ("When they ran out of wine, the mother of Jesus said to him, 'They have no wine'") is at least a hint that Jesus should use his miraculous powers to resolve this problem. Is there a touch of maternal pride here?

Our Lord's response to his mother seems harsh to our ear: "Woman, what does your concern have to do with me?" If a man were to address his mother in this manner in our society it would be regarded as disrespectful. At that time, however, this idiomatic expression carried no hint of disrespect and was entirely honourable.[45] We should also recognise that this was a private exchange between a mother and son, not a public rebuke. It was necessary for Jesus to assert his authority in determining his actions. It is obvious that Mary did not feel slighted, and her abundant confidence in her son is seen in verse 5 where she commanded the servants to do as he instructed – a message that all servants might do well to heed. If the Lord asks us to do something we should comply without question.

In verse 12, after the wedding in Cana, we see Mary and her other children travelling with Jesus and his disciples to Capernaum: "After this he went down to Capernaum, he, his mother, his brothers, and his disciples; and they did not stay there many days". No reason is given for the short stay in Capernaum, but it may have been because they were uncomfortable about the attention Jesus was starting to attract. At least at certain times in his ministry Mary was with her son. At other times family commitments appear to have restricted her ability to travel.

Back to Nazareth?

It would seem that at least several members of the Lord's family either remained in Nazareth or returned to the town from Capernaum. Did they find it uncomfortable being in such close proximity to Jesus as opposition to his ministry intensified? One can imagine

45 – See Clara Lucas Balfour, *The Women of Scripture*, page 254.

Mary being particularly anxious about her firstborn son, especially in the light of the unique circumstances that surrounded his birth. Perhaps this is why John says that they did not stay long at Capernaum.

Although we cannot be certain, it seems likely that most if not all of the family gravitated back to Nazareth – obscure, off the beaten track, quiet and isolated from the growing tension associated with the public ministry of their son and half-brother. When Jesus visited Nazareth the townsfolk referred by name to his family members: his sisters in particular in terms which must mean they lived in the village (see Matthew 13:54-57). We may discern from this passage that Mary had at least seven children; in addition to Jesus there were sons named James, Joses, Simon and Judas and at least two daughters, for the plural "sisters" is used by the townsfolk.

Fanatical worshippers of Mary, with their cult of perpetual virginity, cannot accept that Mary had other children so they suppose that references to Jesus' siblings must refer to children Joseph had sired in a previous marriage. We may be certain that Mary had other children through Joseph, however, because any that Joseph had sired earlier would be older than Jesus and not as likely to be linked so closely to Mary.

The passage in Matthew 13 suggests a number of interesting facts about Mary and Jesus. His neighbours regard him as the carpenter's son (verse 55). Mary and Joseph had either not told their neighbours the truth about the begettal of Jesus, or they had not been believed if they did. It is possible that they did not even tell their own children. It is also evident that the advanced spiritual understanding that Jesus had demonstrated in discussion with the doctors in Jerusalem when he was 12 had not been so openly paraded in Nazareth – hence the incredulity in their cry: "Where did this man get this wisdom, and these mighty works?" (verse 54). His long years of preparation in Nazareth had been spent quietly and unobtrusively – neither he nor Mary had ever sought to promote themselves. They lived humble lives waiting for God's timetable.

While it is clear that there were times when Mary accompanied her son in his ministry, there appear to have been other times when she pulled back. This may have been so she could attend to her maternal duties, perhaps for instance to assist when grandchildren were born. There were, however, times when Mary was wary about the course Jesus was taking. On one recorded occasion Mary and her children came to speak with Jesus:

> "(Jesus) went into a house. But again the crowd assembled, so that there was no opportunity for them even to snatch a meal. Hearing of this, his relatives ('kinsmen', AV margin – including Mary?) came from home to take him by force, for they said, 'He is out of his mind.'" (Mark 3:20,21, Weymouth)

They were concerned that Jesus had taken leave of his senses. It would be only natural in such circumstances for those who loved him to intervene, even to the point of forcibly removing him from danger. His family may have been concerned that the way Jesus was conducting himself would cause him to suffer at the hands of the corrupt Jewish leaders. Given the evident corruption of the Jewish leadership, so often exposed by her son, this must have seemed highly likely. Mark makes it clear that the scribes were also saying Jesus was mad or demon possessed (verse 22 and 30), and they could well use this as a pretext to act against him. In every respect, then, this was an expression of the entirely natural concern of a loving mother for her firstborn son, even though her perspective on that occasion was wrong:

> "Then his brothers and his mother came, and standing outside they sent to him, calling him. And a multitude was sitting around him; and they said to him, 'Look, your mother and your brothers are outside seeking you.'" (Mark 3:31,32)

Mark is careful to set the scene; Jesus is inside preaching but his mother and brothers were not in the room. Why were they outside rather than inside supporting him? It may simply be because the room was too crowded and they could not enter (see verse 20). Alternatively it may have been a reflection of their growing nervousness about his mission. He was incurring the wrath of some very vicious and powerful men. Mary would be aware of the campaign they had launched to undermine him. They would need hardly any excuse to arrest him and, as became only too plain later, they were willing to use violence if necessary to protect their position.

Whatever the motive, again the Lord Jesus had to correct his mother's misperception. He was her firstborn son, but that could not distract him from the vital work he had to do as Messiah. Family links can never override spiritual obligations, and Jesus used this incident to demonstrate that that was so for all his followers:

"He answered them, saying, 'Who is my mother, or my brothers?' And he looked around in a circle at those who sat about him, and said, 'Here are my mother and my brothers! For whoever does the will of God is my brother and my sister and mother.'"

(Mark 3:33-35)

"Yes, a sword shall pierce through your own soul also", Simeon had said, and here was a case where Mary's heart was pierced. It would be wrong, however, to read the Lord's comment as repudiation of maternal affection or of disregard for his mother's welfare and feelings. No one was more conscious than Jesus of just how much Mary had suffered in doing 'the will of my Father'. There was no sense in which he was calling into question her status as his mother and her right to receive honour and respect. It was merely a case of clarifying priorities. In fact Jesus in Matthew 19:19 specifically confirmed the importance of the command to honour father and mother.

A stranger to his mother's children
We know from several passages that the Lord's brothers did not believe in him. Presumably their support of their mother in the incident recorded in Mark 3 was motivated by respect for Mary rather than devotion to their brother. In John 7 they challenged him directly, and John's blunt comment summarises the situation very clearly: "even his brothers did not believe in him" (John 7:5). The Lord's response to their unbelief is very poignant: "Then Jesus said to them, 'My time has not yet come, but your time is always ready'" (verse 6). Was he suggesting that when they were ready to believe he would be ready to receive them? That certainly is the case today with his spiritual brothers and sisters and we rejoice that it is so, although we must never presume upon the fact.

There is a very sad statement in the messianic Psalm 69 which expresses the anguish of our Lord at the disbelief of his brothers:

"Because for your sake I have borne reproach; shame has covered my face. I have become a stranger to my brothers, and an alien to my mother's children; because zeal for your house has eaten me up, and the reproaches of those who reproach you have fallen on me." (Psalm 69:7-9)

Our Lord's devotion to his heavenly Father alienated him from his earthly siblings. They were unwilling to share his reproach any more than was necessary. This must have been a source of great anguish to Mary. No mother likes to see division among her children and no loving son would wish to be the cause of family tension and of heartache for his mother. Here was another example of the truth of Simeon's words: "Yes, a sword shall pierce through your own soul also".

"Blessed is the womb that bore you"
There came a day in the Lord's ministry when "he steadfastly set his face to go to Jerusalem" (Luke 9:51) to be crucified. The whispering campaign suggesting

that Jesus was demon possessed or mad had continued. In Luke 11 when, as he trod the road to Jerusalem, the Lord healed a poor wretch who could not speak he was accused of being an agent of Beelzebub. He responded to this outrageous claim with the parable of the strong man spoiled and the parable of the unoccupied house.

The vicious innuendo of the Jewish rulers could not overcome the faithful response of certain ordinary people, and one woman who witnessed these events was particularly affected:

"It happened, as he spoke these things, that a certain woman from the crowd raised her voice and said to him, 'Blessed is the womb that bore you, and the breasts which nursed you!' But he said, 'More than that, blessed are those who hear the word of God and keep it!'" (Luke 11:27,28)

To a man who dearly loved his mother and who knew her suffering as the handmaid of the Lord this might have been a very welcome endorsement. And indeed Mary is blessed as Gabriel and Elizabeth had said. But our Lord did not allow this otherwise truthful saying to divert him from delivering an important message in response. Mary was blessed, but it was because she had meekly submitted to the word of God as conveyed by Gabriel. And the same is true for all the servants of God. It is our response to God's word that determines whether we are blessed. Outbursts of emotion in relation to Mary, Jesus or even those directed towards God – no matter how heartfelt and genuine – are no substitute for devotion to the will of God as expressed in his word.

In the shadow of the cross

The next reference to Mary in the record is the most poignant incident in her life. In John's record of the crucifixion we see Mary at the foot of the cross. This scene is agonising, not just in respect of the agony of our Lord as he hung upon the cross, but also in respect of the anguish of Mary as she witnessed the evil act. Simeon's words had never been more apt. Mary must have felt every nail, mourned every indignity and shared every taunt. But she could not leave her son at this hour:

"Now there stood by the cross of Jesus his mother, and his mother's sister, Mary the wife of Clopas, and Mary Magdalene. When Jesus therefore saw his mother, and the disciple whom he loved standing by, he said to his mother, 'Woman, behold your son!' Then he said to the disciple, 'Behold your mother!' And from that hour that disciple took her to his own home." (John 19:25-27)

Think what a blessing this was for our Lord. In her late forties Mary was now a very aged women by the standards of the time. Most men and women have to suffer the death of their mother before they die. But Mary's life had been spared and she was there to be a comfort to her son. Most of those who had been close to Jesus had fled, but not Mary. Her heart must have ached but she could not abandon him. She would share the shame of his nakedness. She would thirst with Jesus as he thirsted. More than most Israelite women, as the wife and mother of carpenters, Mary would have had an insight into the power involved in driving those nails into her son's feet and hands. She would understand more than most what this meant for the victim.

As she witnessed her son's agony Mary's mind, which had so often been exercised as she thought about her son and his mission (Luke 1:29 and 2:19), must have been full of recollections about Jesus. The anxious circumstances of his birth, alone in an unwelcoming town; the wonder of the visits from the shepherds and the wise men; the hurried flight into Egypt; the anguish of the slaughter of the innocents; the idyllic childhood in Nazareth; the worrying search for a twelve-year old youth in Jerusalem; the loving support she received after Joseph's death; the mixed emotions with which she observed his public ministry: all these and many others must have flooded into her mind as she watched the agony of her firstborn.

The hour that had not come at Cana had now arrived. It is true that "greater love has no one than this, than to lay down one's life for his friends" (John 15:13), but even in the agony of that act our Lord manifested his very special love for his mother in a personal expression of concern. Even as his life ebbed from him, his body racked with pain, our Lord was touched by the suffering of the one with whom his life had been so intimately entwined. He knew what pain she must be experiencing as she watched this violent crime unfold. He knew the great sense of emptiness that might envelop her in the next few days. Yes, he knew that when he was resurrected she would rejoice perhaps more than anyone else, but there were ahead the painful days between his death and resurrection, not to mention her declining years after his ascension to Heaven, when she would need practical support.

Standing with his mother was John – his own cousin and one of the inner circle of disciples. John was a man of great passion and love, as well as a man of some means. To whom better could he entrust his mother's care? Tenderly, in spite of abject pain, he addresses Mary (again as "Woman"), "behold your son!" – behold John beside you; he will look after you.[46] Had he arranged this prior to his arrest? Perhaps he had. Certainly Jesus had confided in John that he was about to be betrayed. While reclining next to John in the upper room Jesus might also have made arrangements for his mother's welfare. Now he seals the

---

46 – An alternative approach is to read "behold your son" as intended to direct Mary to consider her son on the cross, fulfilling the task for which he had been born. Jesus would have known what was going through his mother's mind; perhaps recognising that the ignominy and pain he was now enduring was the very reason he had been provided may would help her cope with the agony she felt in her heart as a mother. The Lord's words "It is finished" (John 19:30) uttered shortly afterwards could be read as being consistent with this sentiment.

arrangements: it is an act of love towards two for whom Jesus had particular affection:

"Two hearts sought each other in the growing darkness; a heart bleeding from a sword thrust found strength in the kinship of a disciple who loved; a heart broken with grief found solace in a solemn trust".[47]

John accepted without hesitation the commission in verse 27 (there is an example here that all the disciples of the Lord should follow). Why was it necessary for John to take on this role? Mary had other children. Why wouldn't they be responsible for the care of their ageing widowed mother? In 1 Timothy 5:4 and 16 the Apostle Paul explained the responsibility of families for the care of widows:

"If a widow has children or grandchildren, let these learn first to show piety towards their own homes and to prove their gratitude to their parents; for this is well pleasing in the sight of God ... If a believing woman has widows dependent on her, she should relieve their wants, and save the Church from being burdened." (Weymouth)

The key point here may be the reference to those who believe assuming responsibility for the care of widows. We can only speculate, but as we have seen, at least some of Mary's other children had not yet embraced their brother as Messiah. Until they were converted they might not have provided an appropriate level of spiritual support for Mary, even if they could provide for her natural needs. Was the commissioning of John to become Mary's guardian designed to make his half-brothers and half-sisters think about their own personal situation and revisit their conclusions about Jesus? Perhaps it was. In any event, it would appear from Matthew 13 that those who had homes, particularly his sisters, were in Nazareth, whereas it is likely that John had access to accommodation in

47 – Melva Purkis, *A Life of Jesus*, 3rd edition, page 334.

Jerusalem[48] and in both a spiritual and practical sense could care for Mary from that very day. Whatever the reason, Mary and John formed a bond at the foot of the cross and must have strengthened one another as they watched life ebb from Jesus. John took Mary to himself and no doubt they mourned together.

As Mary returned to the home of John that evening her heart must have ached and her mind must have been spinning. Just a few days before, multitudes had hailed her son as Messiah as he rode into Jerusalem. From that height of joy and anticipation she had plunged to a depth of sadness greater than she had ever experienced in her difficult life. We do not know what she made of the tragic scene as she watched her beloved firstborn writhing in pain and humiliation on the stake. We do not know what torments racked her brain as she sought rest that night and as she weathered the days between the crucifixion and the resurrection. In her fictional work, *A Time to See*, S. J. Knight speculates that "her mute cries for answers from his Father went unvoiced, because the woman who had once been overshadowed by the power of the Holy Spirit, knew that she did not need to understand; it was enough for her to accept. *Faith*! Without it, life was death anyway. But none of this washed away the pain, the confusion, the reaction, the shock."[49]

In John 20:2 the apostle John accompanied Peter to the tomb of Jesus on the first day of the week. They found it empty. John immediately grasped the significance:

"Then the other disciple, who had been the first to come to the tomb, also went in and saw and was convinced. For until now they had not understood the

48 – John appears to have come from an affluent family. His father had hired servants (Mark 1:20) and it would seem that his family mixed in highly placed circles in Jerusalem because he had access to the house of the High Priest (John 18:15). In these circumstances it is possible that in addition to a home in Galilee his family had a home in Jerusalem.
49 – S. J. Knight, *A Time to See*, page 534.

inspired teaching, that He must rise again from among the dead. Then they went away and returned home." (John 20:8-10, Weymouth)

In spite of what Jesus had told his apostles they had not expected the resurrection of Jesus because they had not fully appreciated the scriptural teaching about his resurrection. But John immediately perceived the significance of what he saw. And in verse 10 he went home. Who was at home waiting for news of the tomb? Mary! How she must have thrilled at the news, and how many of those sayings she had treasured up over so many years must now have come to life. Mary had pondered them, turning them over and over in her mind, the earliest of them for thirty-four years; now many of them started to make sense. So many pieces of the puzzles that racked her brain suddenly fell into place.

We can only begin to imagine Mary's unbridled joy as she greeted this news and later as she actually saw her son raised from the grave. At this time Mary, after many years of suffering, realised like she had never before the truth of the prophecy of Elizabeth: "blessed (happy) are you among women" (Luke 1:42). We are not told anything about Mary's first meeting with her resurrected son. One author has suggested a reason for this:

"There is one picture which is not recorded for us in the Gospels. It is the meeting of Jesus with his mother after his resurrection. I used to wonder why this is not mentioned. I do not wonder now. I think this meeting would probably take place in the privacy of Mary's room in John's home, and would be too sacred for other human eyes; too intimate and too tender for even the sympathetic and understanding ears of Luke, the 'beloved physician,' to whom we are indebted for most of the information we have concerning Mary."[50]

---

50 – Lilian Adams, *The Testimony*, Volume 10 (1940), page 100.

10

EPILOGUE

"These all continued with one accord in prayer and supplication ..."   (Acts 1:14)

THE final reference in scripture to Mary is in Acts chapter 1:

"Then they (the apostles) returned to Jerusalem from the mount called Olivet, which is near Jerusalem, a Sabbath day's journey. And when they had entered, they went up into the upper room where they were staying: Peter, James, John, and Andrew; Philip and Thomas; Bartholomew and Matthew; James the son of Alphaeus and Simon the Zealot; and Judas the son of James. These all continued with one accord in prayer and supplication, with the women and Mary the mother of Jesus, and with his brothers."   (verses 12-14)

This, the only reference to Mary after the Lord's ascension, is suitably understated. One single sentence is all that we have about the remainder of her life. No fuss is made of Mary; no special status is assigned to her. She is mentioned neither first nor last in the list, just one of the faithful, continuing with one accord in prayer and supplication. Her supplications very likely had a special intensity in view of the circumstances but they are presented as no more important than those of the others.

The reference to our Lord's brothers suggests that the crucifixion had a powerful influence on them, overpowering their earlier disbelief. This must have added to Mary's joy and contentment as she celebrated the resurrection of her son. It seems appropriate that our last glimpse of Mary this side of our Lord's return is of a woman joined in prayer with other faithful saints. We first met Mary as a devout teenager in Galilee and as we take our leave of her she is a devout grandmother living with John and worshipping with the apostles.

Did Mary continue to live in Jerusalem with John, or did she eventually return to her other children in Nazareth? We cannot be certain. Both Nazareth and Jerusalem must have been places about which Mary would have mixed feelings. In all the references to John in Acts he is a resident of Jerusalem. The only reference to John outside of Acts and the books attributed to him is in Galatians 2:1-9, where it is also stated that he dwelt in Jerusalem. Did he stay with Mary in her declining years until she fell asleep? Again, we cannot be certain. All that has been revealed is that Mary and her children were united with the brothers and sisters who constituted the ecclesia of the living God waiting for the return of her son from Heaven.

It is hoped these thoughts have helped the reader to come to know Mary a little better. She is a wonderful example for all, and especially for the young, for mothers, for those who have known poverty, for those who have suffered for their faithfulness, for those who know the anguish of a divided household, for those who have lost a son. In short, she is an inspiration to all who would serve their God with their whole heart, mind and soul.

It is sad that the errors of an apostate system might at times have diminished our regard for her. In recognising these errors about Mary for what they are, however, we must not fail to observe that the Bible does ascribe to her an exalted status. "We must give Mary her due. We must not allow ourselves to entertain a grudge against the mother of our Lord because some enthusiasts for her have given her more than her due."[51] The mother of our Lord Jesus Christ was not

---

51 – Alexander Whyte, *Bible Characters Joseph and Mary to James, the Lord's Brother*, page 7.

immaculate and she is not now in heaven; Mary is nevertheless "blessed" and "highly favoured".

"We find in Mary a noble woman, fit for the great calling that came to her; a woman genuine and selfless, of great strength of character and power of endurance. But she is truly woman, with human limitations, sometimes uncomprehending and having to suffer rebuke. She had to experience a growing separation from her Son, only to be brought to him at last with fuller understanding, a tested faith and a loftier love. This is no unearthly and immaculate being but a real woman capable of error, but rising to heights of love. She is blessed indeed above women, and happy will she be in that joy which will be hers for ever at her Son's return."[52]

Mary is an inspiring woman who deserves our admiration. She occupies a central role in God's plan of reconciliation for perishing mankind. She is a focal point for many of the promises of God in the Old Testament, while at a personal level she is an excellent role-model for all the faithful. We would do well to capture a measure of her steadfast faith and commitment.

---

52 – L. G. Sargent, *The Christadelphian*, Volume 95 (1958), page 398.

11

APPENDIX –
MARIOLATRY

GAUSSEN in his work on the plenary inspiration of the scriptures makes the point that one of the evidences of the inspiration of the Biblical record is the fact that historical material is recorded in a manner that was designed to prevent false conclusions being drawn. He illustrates his point by reference to the circumspection with which authors of the Gospel records refer to Mary:

"What divine foresight, and what prophetical wisdom, both in their narratives and in their expressions! How readily might they have been led, in their ardent adoration of the Son, to express themselves, when speaking of the mother, in terms of too much reverence! Would not a single word, suffered to escape from the want of circumspection so natural to their first emotions, have for ever sanctioned the idolatries of future ages towards Mary, and the crime of the worship which is paid to her?"[53]

Sadly, in spite of the lack of such loose language in the record, an unjustified and discrediting worship of Mary developed as the Church abandoned the purity of apostolic doctrine.

Mariolatry (literally, 'the worship of Mary'), a hallmark of Roman Catholicism but also a feature in other systems, has its roots in ancient, pre-Biblical times. Alexander Hislop's well-known book *The Two Babylons*[54] traces the origin of Roman Catholic

---

53 – L. Gaussen, *Theopneustia: The Plenary Inspiration of the Holy Scriptures* (transl. David Scott), C. J. Thynne, London, page 302.
54 – Alexander Hislop, *The Two Babylons*, S. W. Partridge & Co., London.

teachings and is subtitled, "The Papal Worship proved to be the Worship of Nimrod and his Wife". Hislop emphasises the importance in both systems of the worship of mother and child, an image so very prominent in Roman Catholic art and imagery.

The Roman Catholic church recognises a three-level hierarchy of adoration:

- *Latria* – the adoration due to God alone (which in that Trinitarian system includes the Lord Jesus Christ) and given on account of His supremacy;
- *Hyperdulia* – worship offered to Mary on account of her 'maternity of God', her other eminent gifts and her supereminent sanctity; and
- *Dulia* – worship offered to saints on account of their sanctity.

While this three-level approach to adoration suggests a clear recognition of the supremacy of God, the practice is not quite so clear. An illustration of the strength of Roman Catholic devotion to Mary is found in the fact that the Church has established 22 separate festivals annually in honour of Jesus Christ and 42 in honour of Mary. In addition, the months of May and October are given over to the worship of the Virgin, while every Saturday not appropriated to another purpose is devoted to Mary.

Ishtar, Astarte and Aphrodite

Throughout the ancient Middle East and eastern Mediterranean the cult of the mother-goddess was pervasive. It took various forms and a range of names was attributed to the central figure; Ishtar and Astarte are two of the better-known names. The Greek version of the cult involved the worship of Aphrodite.

Temples and shrines to Aphrodite were established throughout the Hellenic regions. In Cyprus the main centre of the cult of Aphrodite was Palaepaphos ('Old Paphos'), near the modern city of Paphos. Ancient legends claimed that Aphrodite was born from the sea foam on the coast near this city.

The extensive ruins of Palaepaphos are today a major tourist attraction. In ancient times the city was well known for its annual festival in honour of Aphrodite which involved processions, music, dancing and banqueting. It also involved ritual prostitution. Titus, the Roman general who overthrew Jerusalem in AD70, visited the oracle of Aphrodite at this place the year before his conquest of Jerusalem and was emboldened by what he understood to be the oracle's prediction of a great future.

The cult of Aphrodite persisted until the fourth century when the Roman Emperor Theodosius (AD 379-395) ordered all pagan shrines and temples, including those connected with Aphrodite at Palaepaphos, to close. By this time, however, the Christian church had already been corrupted by paganism and the cult of Aphrodite was adapted to that of Mary. An example of this is evident at Palaepaphos, where immediately adjacent to the shrine of Aphrodite a church honouring Mary was erected after the proscription of the pagan temples. Known as the church of Panayia Galatariotissa (the milk-giving virgin), it became a shrine to which young mothers having difficulty nursing their babies could resort to beseech Mary's assistance.[55]

Mary and the Eastern Orthodox Churches

Although it is common in Protestant societies to associate the worship of Mary with Roman Catholicism, it is obvious from the example of the church of Panayia Galatariotissa at Palaepaphos that it also pervades the Eastern Orthodox churches. These churches honour and venerate Mary as 'more honourable than the Cherubim and more glorious without compare than the Seraphim'. Mary is mentioned by name in every service and her intercession before God is sought. It should be noted, however, that in the Orthodox view Mary is not regarded as a mediatrix or co-redemptress. They regard

55 – See Tony Benson, *The Testimony*, October 2007, page XVIII.

Mary only as an intercessor (the teaching of 1 Timothy 2:5 notwithstanding), and the content of prayer addressed to her is a request for her intercession.

Orthodox theologians read into the Biblical text interpretations that bolster their preconceived ideas about Mary. For example:

- The Lord's instruction to John from the cross "Behold your mother!" (John 19:27) is read not as an instruction to an individual to discharge a duty of care to a grieving widow but as a declaration that his mother should be regarded as the mother of all Christians.
- The vision of Jacob's ladder (Genesis 28:12) is taken as a prophecy of Mary being the means by which God (in the form of the Trinitarian God the Son) would enter the world.
- Ezekiel is said to have prophesied of Mary's perpetual virginity when he wrote: "This gate shall be shut; it shall not be opened, and no man shall enter by it, because the LORD God of Israel has entered by it; therefore it shall be shut" (Ezekiel 44:2). This interpretation obliges them to deny that Mary and Joseph consummated their marriage and produced the brothers and sisters of the Lord to which the record refers.
- The burning bush seen by Moses (Exodus 3) is said to prefigure the way in which Mary would carry in her womb the God-man, Jesus Christ, the God who is a consuming fire, without herself being consumed.

Eclectic ideas

There is a certain irony in the appropriation to Mary of the licentious worship of Aphrodite. At about the same time this was occurring, the myth of Mary's perpetual virginity, which had first been propounded in the apocryphal Book of James (also known by the title *Protevangelium Jacobi* and believed to have been written in the mid second century) began to be widely accepted within the corrupted Christian church. Yet even that work does not suggest that adoration should be offered to Mary.

Also dating from ancient times is the belief that, sometime after the crucifixion and ascension of her son into heaven, Mary moved with John (to whom her welfare had been entrusted by Jesus) to Ephesus. Tourists to Ephesus today are shown a small building which is claimed to be Mary's home in her old age. This is in spite of the fact that the cottage almost certainly does not date from the first century and that there is absolutely no evidence that Mary ever lived in Ephesus.

The blending of pagan beliefs with the worship of Mary was not just a feature of the period following the rise of Constantine when corrupted Christianity was displacing the polytheistic religious systems of the Roman Empire. When Roman Catholic missionaries took their religion to the new world the idols of the indigenous inhabitants were often linked to Mary and other saints, presumably to assist them to transition to the new system. In Mexico, for example, Roman Catholics acknowledge as the nation's patron saint the Virgin of Guadalupe. Even today, many Mexican Indians venerate the Virgin of Guadalupe as an Aztec goddess.

Mother of God

Ancient though it may be, Roman Catholic worship of Mary has continued to evolve. The term 'mother of God' began to be used of Mary fairly commonly in the fifth century, having first appeared in writing in a work entitled 'Transitus Mariae' in the fourth century. In that work all created things are called upon to adore Mary. The author says that Mary was 'holy and elect of God before she was born'.

The Councils of Ephesus (431) and Chalcedon (451) endorsed the use of the title 'Theotokus' (Greek, 'God-bearer', or 'the one who gives birth to God') for Mary. Her identity and status as 'Theotokos' is considered by both the Roman Catholic and the Eastern Orthodox

Churches as indispensable and is defined as official dogma. The only other Mariological teaching so defined by both churches is that of her virginity. Certain other Roman Catholic Marian beliefs, however, (e.g., Mary's sinlessness, the circumstances surrounding her conception and birth, and her continuing virginity following the birth of Jesus) while taught and believed by the Orthodox Church and expressed in its liturgy and writings, are not formally defined by the Eastern Orthodox Churches and belief in them is not considered a precondition for baptism within those communions.

The adoration of Mary came to even more considerable prominence under Pope Gregory the Great (AD 590-604) and, at least in Roman Catholic and Eastern Orthodox circles, has been prominent ever since.

In the sixth century the doctrine of the bodily assumption of Mary to heaven began to be developed. Celebration of this event spread fairly widely even though the doctrine was only given official endorsement in 1950 when Pope Pius XII formally proclaimed that Mary ascended into Heaven to be bodily with her son and to reign as Queen of Heaven. Pius' declaration was made in spite of Jeremiah's strident condemnation of Israel's false worship of the Queen of Heaven:

"The children gather wood, the fathers kindle the fire, and the women knead dough, to make cakes for the queen of heaven; and they pour out drink offerings to other gods, that they may provoke me to anger." (Jeremiah 7:18)

The concept of cakes prepared for the Queen of Heaven found a remarkably direct fulfilment in relation to Mary in the practices of the Collyridians, a fourth century sect in the Middle East comprised possibly exclusively of women who literally offered cakes to the Virgin Mary. This sect saw Mary as a divine being and for that reason denied that her marriage with Joseph was ever consummated, and thus that she had no children other than Jesus. They met once a year to offer small round cakes (Greek, *collyra,* from which the name of the sect is derived) as a means of honouring Mary as a goddess. It was suggested by Neander that this practice was a corruption of the communion meal; others have suggested that it was an adaptation of the pagan worship of Ceres which involved the offering of bread. Either way there is a striking parallel with the words of Jeremiah.

In the tenth century the worship of Mary reached new excesses. A custom developed in which people abstained from flesh and Mass was celebrated on Saturdays in honour of Mary. It is in this century that we have the earliest evidence of the special Marian prayers known as the rosary and the Crown of St Mary.

The rosary is a series of prayers devout Catholics often recite: it involves saying the Ave Maria (see below for details of this prayer) 150 times in 15 groups of 10, with a version of the Lord's Prayer in between each group of 10. The Crown of St Mary is a devotion which consists of six or seven repetitions of the Lord's Prayer combined with 60 or 70 salutations to Mary. One can see where the balance lies in this devotion!

Immaculate Conception

In the twelfth century there was a vigorous debate about the possibility of Mary being untainted by original or hereditary sin. A theologian as respected as Thomas Aquinas declared quite vehemently that such a theory was impossible and the concept was rejected. This fact, however, did not stop Pope Pius IX in 1854 reversing that outcome and proclaiming the doctrine of the Immaculate Conception. That doctrine teaches that, by some miracle, Mary was free from the guilt of original sin.

In the thirteenth century Goivanni di Fidanza (about 1222-1274), a theologian later canonised as St Bonaventura, prepared a Psalter in honour of Mary. The preface of that Psalter commences with the words: 'Come unto Mary, all ye that are weary and heavy laden, and she will give you rest'. His blasphemous mishandling of the word of God did not end with the preface. In his Psalter each of the 150 Psalms is changed to make them address the Virgin Mary rather than Almighty God, as the following examples illustrate:

Psalm	NKJV	Bonaventura's Paraphrase
51:1	"Have mercy upon me, O God, according to your loving-kindness; according to the multitude of your tender mercies, blot out my transgressions."	"Have mercy on me, O Lady, who art called the Mother of Mercy; according to thy tender mercy; cleanse me from my iniquities."
84:1	"How lovely is your tabernacle, O LORD of hosts!"	"How amiable are thy tabernacles, O Queen of Virtue!"
95:1	"Oh come, let us sing to the LORD! Let us shout joyfully to the Rock of our salvation."	"O come, let us sing unto our Lady: let us heartily rejoice in the Virgin that brings us salvation."

In the fifteenth century St Bernardino of Siena (1380-1444) is credited with further blasphemies about the Virgin Mary, including the following egregious statements:[56]

- All things, even God, are servants of the empire of the Virgin.
- All the angelic spirits are the ministers and servants of this glorious Virgin.
- God is subject to the command of Mary.
- To comprise all in a brief (sic) sentence, I have no doubt that God granted all the pardons and

---

56 – Quoted by H. W. Dearden, *Modern Romanism Examined*, pages 225-226. Chas. Thynne & Jarvis Ltd., London 1927.

liberations in the Old Testament on account of His love and reverence for this blessed maid, by which God pre-ordained from eternity that she should, by predestination, be honoured above all His works.

• Mary has done more for God than God has for man; so that thus, on account of the Blessed Virgin (whom nevertheless He Himself made), God is in a certain manner under greater obligations to us than we are to Him.

In the religious celebration known as the Office of the Immaculate Conception (first nocturn, third lesson) reference is made to Genesis 3:15 but it is mistranslated to make it apply to Mary, '*She* shall bruise your head, and you shall bruise *her* heel'. Thus they appropriate to Mary that which God ascribed to her son.

Apparitions of Mary

Most non-Roman Catholics have little idea of just how excessive is the veneration of Mary in Roman Catholicism. A D Norris, in an interesting article about Mariolatry in *The Christadelphian* in 1992,[57] described the idolatry surrounding Mary at Lourdes in France, where Mary is alleged to have appeared 18 separate times in 1858 to a peasant girl later canonised as St. Bernadette.

Lourdes has been become famous for what are said to be miraculous healings and is visited by many pilgrims seeking cures. In the chapel at this shrine there is a mosaic of Mary with her arms extended and with words around her head that translate as 'Through Mary to Jesus'. This is a reference to Roman Catholic teaching about her role as a mediatrix between Jesus and sinners. That concept is enshrined in the well known Ave Maria prayer, a common prayer for Catholics, which uses these words:

---

57 – A. D. Norris, 'Hail, thou art highly favoured', *The Christadelphian*, Volume 129 (1992), pages 455 to 457.

"Hail, Mary, full of grace! The Lord is with thee. Blessed art thou above all women, and blessed is Jesus, the fruit of thy womb. Holy Mary, Mother of God, pray for us sinners, both now and in the hour of our death. Amen."

There are several other famous sites where Mary is said to have appeared to people, including Fatima in Portugal, where the Virgin is said to have appeared in 1917 to three illiterate children, and at Medjugorje in Bosnia and Herzegovina, where Mary is claimed to have appeared to six young children in 1981.

Protestant veneration of Mary

Even in some so-called Protestant churches there are excesses of Mary worship. In the English reformation there was a widespread reaction against Mary as a mediatrix alongside Christ. That teaching was rejected by the Church of England as was any overt devotion to Mary.

Prior to the reformation there had been sites of Marian pilgrimage in many places, including in England. Such practices were actively discouraged in those countries where Protestantism held sway. In the nineteenth century, under the influence of the Oxford Movement, attitudes towards her started to change. In 1922 the erection of a new statue of Our Lady of Walsingham in England reignited Anglican interest in a revival of the pre-reformation pilgrimage to that spot and from the early 1930s Walsingham became a centre for Anglican as well as Catholic Marian pilgrims.

At Yankalilla in South Australia there is an Anglican church where it is claimed there is an apparition of Mary on the wall and this attracts interest from pilgrims. Just how anyone could know what she looks like is hard to tell, but the gullible seem willing to assume that markings more likely attributable to rising damp, mildew or some other natural explanation constitute an image of Mary.

Mary acquired a new prominence in Anglican worship through the liturgical renewals of the twentieth century. In most Anglican prayer books, Mary is again mentioned by name in the liturgical prayers. Further, 15 August (when Roman Catholics celebrate the assumption of Mary to Heaven) has come to be celebrated by devout Anglicans as a feast in honour of Mary. Other pre-reformation feasts associated with Mary have also been renewed. Within the Anglican Communion there is a devotional society, the Society of Mary, dedicated to honouring Mary and which operates in both the United Kingdom and the United States.

Modern apparitions

It might be expected that apparitions of Mary would be associated only with superstitious times and unsophisticated societies. Not so. In 2006 a woman in New Zealand found a pebble bearing the apparent image of the Virgin Mary at Kaikoura's South Beach.[58] The media reported that friends told her the pebble could be worth a lot of money, but the finder said she wanted to keep the pebble as a good-luck charm, suggesting a superstitious mindset. The finder was quoted as saying "I got it and I started having an awesome run of luck". The prospect of financial gain must have overcome her need for luck because in 2007 she attempted to auction the pebble, hoping to make at least $NZ70,000!

The United States has also been the location of many 'sightings' of Mary, with Americans claiming to have seen her image in places such as a garage door and a lemon slice in a bar. An American woman once paid $US28,000 for a ten-year old toasted cheese sandwich with an image of Mary pressed into its crusty top! It is sad that such superstitious delusions have detracted from the honour that really does belong to the handmaid of the Lord.

---

58 – *The Press* (New Zealand), 24 October 2007.

Mary in Islam

Inordinate adoration of Mary is not restricted to corrupted Christianity. Muslims also venerate Mary. In the Qur'an, no woman is given more attention than Mary; references to her are more frequent in the Qur'an than they are in the New Testament. She is the only woman specifically named in the Qur'an and is one of only eight people who have one of the Qur'an's 114 Suras named after them: the nineteenth Surah is named Mariam (Mary in Arabic). The third Surah is named after her father, Imran (not a name found in either of the genealogies of the Lord in Matthew and Luke). Mary plays a very significant role in Islam and she is regarded as an example and a sign for all people (Surah 21:91).

The Qur'an records extensive details about Mary, many of which vary significantly from the biblical record. It says that Mary is of the tribe of Levi rather than Judah (Surah 19:28), while Joseph, the wise men, and manger are not mentioned anywhere. Mary is said to have given birth to Jesus at the base of a palm tree in a remote place (Surah 19:22-27). What the Qur'an records about Mary often is quite fanciful and has an air of unreality. John Thorpe has demonstrated that the origin of several of these fanciful stories may be traced to apocryphal works from the centuries between the time of Jesus and Mohammed.[59]

Moslems recognise Mary as a person of special qualities and regard the conception of Jesus as miraculous (Surah 19:16-21). They do not, however, regard Jesus as the Son of God. They argue that, although God can do all things, He only does things that are consistent with His fundamental nature and values: in their view, begetting a son is not consistent with God's nature (Surah 19:92 and 19:35).

Although they deny that Jesus is God's son, Muslims are scathing about the Bible's record of the Lord's ancestry. One Islamic author has said this about the

59 – John Thorpe, *The Bible and Islam* (first edition), pages 93-100.

genealogies of the Lord as recorded in Matthew and Luke:

"Watch now how the Christian fathers have foisted the incestuous progenies of the Old Testament upon their Lord and Saviour, Jesus Christ, in the New Testament. For a man who had no genealogy, they have manufactured one for him. And what a genealogy! Six adulterers and offsprings of incest are imposed upon this holy man of God. Men and women deserving to be stoned to death according to God's own law, as revealed through Moses, and further to be ostracised and debarred from the House of God for generations (Deuteronomy 23:2). Why should God give a "Father" (Joseph) to his "son" (Jesus)? And why such an ignoble ancestry?"[60]

Clearly the high regard in Islam for Mary does not extend to the Biblical record that tells us about this remarkable woman, nor does it take account of the relationship of this record to the divine promises made by God to Eve, the patriarchs and David.

Throughout Islamic writings many names and titles are ascribed to Mary. For example:

• In Surah 66:12 she is referred to as 'the Qanitin', an Arabic term which can be translated as 'devout' and which implies constant submission to God and dedication to prayer and invocation.

• In Surah 3:43 Mary is referred to by the title 'Sajidah' which can be translated as 'she who prostrates to God in worship'. Some Muslim scholars have claimed that the Islamic form of worship in which the hands, knees and the forehead touch the ground together has been derived from Mary's practice as referred to in this verse.

• Mary is called 'Siddiqah', a word meaning she who has faith, in Surah 5:75.

---

60 – Ahmed Deedat, *Is the Bible God's Word?*, page 52, Islamic Propagation Centre, Birmingham, 1987.

- Mary is referred to as 'Tahirah', meaning 'she who was purified' in Surah 3:42. According to a Hadith (a series of short stories about Mohammed) the devil did not touch Mary when she was born (Nisai 4:331). This claim would seem to reflect in a fashion the erroneous Roman Catholic doctrine of the Immaculate Conception. The same concept finds expression in the title 'Ma'suma', meaning 'she who never sinned' which is applied to Mary in Surah 3:35-36.

There is an elaborate theology in Islam relating to Mary, some of which reflects the erroneous teachings of corrupted Christianity and most of which is at odds with the biblical record.

12

SELECT BIBLIOGRAPHY

Background

Alfred Edersheim, *Sketches of Jewish Social Life in the Days of Christ*, Eerdmans, Grand Rapids, 1974.

Alfred Edersheim, *The Life and Times of Jesus The Messiah*, MacDonald, no date.

S. J. Knight, *A Time to Hear*, The Christadelphian, Birmingham, 2006.

S. J. Knight, *A Time to See*, The Christadelphian, Birmingham, 2009.

William Ramsay, *Was Christ Born at Bethlehem? A Study on the Credibility of St. Luke*, Hodder and Stoughton, London, 1898.

William Ramsay, *The Bearing of Recent Discovery on the Trustworthiness of the New Testament*, Hodder and Stoughton, London, 1915.

The Jewish Encyclopedia, Funk & Wagnalls, 1916.

Character studies

Lilian Adams, 'Mary', *The Testimony*, Volume 10 (1940), pages 94 to 96, 100.

Colin Attridge, *Think on These Things* (Chapter Ten), The Dawn Book Supply, Nottingham, 2007.

Clara Lucas Balfour, *The Women of Scripture*, Houlston and Wright, London, 1860.

Mary Benson, 'The Women of Luke's Gospel', *The Testimony*, Volume 77 (2007), pages 264-268.

Tim Hemingray, 'Mary and John', *The Testimony*, Volume 80 (2010), pages 3-5

Peggy Price, 'Mary, the Mother of Jesus', *Women of the Bible*, The Christadelphian, Birmingham, 1982.

L. G. Sargent, 'The mother of our Lord', *The Christadelphian*, Volume 95 (1958), pages 396 to 398.

J. Alec Swaish, 'Mary the mother of our Lord', *The Testimony*, Volume 48 (1978), pages 397 to 398.

Alexander Whyte, *Bible Characters Joseph and Mary to James, the Lord's Brother*, pages 1 to 9, Oliphant Anderson and Ferrier, London, 1904.

Biblical text

George Booker, *Unto Us a Child is Born ...*, self published, 1984.

F. W. Farrar, *St Luke (Cambridge Bible for Schools and Colleges)*, Cambridge, 1910.

John Martin, *In the Fulness of Time*, Glenlock Bible Camp, 1987.

John Mitchell, 'The Pilgrimage of Jesus (2)', *The Testimony*, Volume 26 (1956), page 110.

Melva Purkis, *A Life of Jesus*, The Christadelphian, Birmingham, 1973.

Robert Roberts, *Nazareth Revisited*, The Christadelphian, Birmingham, 1942.

H. A. Whittaker, *Studies in the Gospels*, Biblia, Cannock, no date.

Christadelphian eJournal of Biblical Interpretation Vol. 2. No. 2. April 2008

Hasting's Bible Dictionary, T & T Clark, Edinburgh, 1920.

Mariolatry

H. W. Dearden, *Modern Romanism Examined*, Chas Thynne & Jarvis Ltd, London 1927

Alexander Hislop, *The Two Babylons*, S. W. Partridge & Co., London, 1976 (first published 1919)

Henry Hart Milman, *History of Latin Christianity*, (Nine Volumes), John Murray, London, 1883.

A. D. Norris, 'Hail, thou art highly favoured', *The Christadelphian*, Volume 129 (1992), pages 455 to 457.

John Thorpe, *The Bible and Islam*, self published, no date. (2nd revised edition published 2008)